"An intimate portrait of what mental health and substance-use recovery can look like by someone who has experienced this process firsthand and come out on the other side. Sarah Huxtable Mohr's odyssey . . . will be of interest to individuals who wish to take seriously the spiritual dimension in their treatment even when modern Western psychology negates the sacred foundations of psychology, or the 'science of the soul,' as it is recognized across the diverse cultures."

—SAMUEL BENDECK SOTILLOS,
author of Dismantling Freud

"*Loving the Present* is a beautifully written and highly relatable book that blends spirituality and the principles of recovery with the joy of being in the now. Sarah Huxtable Mohr enlightens us with her storytelling and reminds us that being in the present can help us overcome the biggest life challenges, including addiction. It's a must-read for anyone interested in the healing arts!"

—KIM PETER NORMAN,
MD, UCSF Weill Institute for Neurosciences

"*Loving the Present* is a gift to every survivor out there, a sojourn of the soul. Suffused with ancient wisdom and enriched by learnings of many faiths. Every word dipped in pain, narrating a tale of triumph and of overcoming odds. Sarah is a warrior and champion for many lost souls; I am humbled and grateful to be part of her journey!"

—FARHA ABBASI, DIRECTOR,
Muslim Mental Health Consortium, Michigan State University

"Sarah utilizes her personal life lessons as her main source of information for finding connections between the world religions and philosophies. Her words move the reader through a variety of experiences both earthly and heavenly while displaying courage in exposing her own foibles and missteps so the reader may benefit through her life's lessons to enhance their own spiritual journey."

—Yassir Chadly,
Shaykh, and Associate Professor, The Graduate Theological Union

"Many people and their families are suffering and seeking a way through the painful effects of mental illness and addiction. Sarah shares diverse spiritual and practical tools to overcome the challenges of this dual disorder. Her work recognizes that mental illness and addictions affect people of diverse backgrounds in various ways, therefore multifaceted approaches are needed. Many thanks to Sarah for sharing her personal and professional insights."

—Aneesah Nadir,
pioneer in the field of Muslim Mental Health Advocacy

Loving the Present

Loving the Present

Sufism, Mindfulness, and Recovery
from Addiction and Mental Illness

SARAH HUXTABLE MOHR

RESOURCE *Publications* · Eugene, Oregon

LOVING THE PRESENT
Sufism, Mindfulness, and Recovery from Addiction and Mental Illness

Resource Publications
An Imprint of Wipf and Stock Publishers
199 W. 8th Ave., Suite 3
Eugene, OR 97401

www.wipfandstock.com

PAPERBACK ISBN: 978-1-6667-3596-3
HARDCOVER ISBN: 978-1-6667-9368-0
EBOOK ISBN: 978-1-6667-9369-7

FEBRUARY 8, 2022 9:31 AM

I dedicate this book in loving gratitude to my parents,
Nancy and Larry Mohr,
without whom nothing would have been possible.

PSALM 91: 1-12

Whoever dwells in the shelter of the Most High
will rest in the shadow of the Almighty.
I will say of the Lord, "He is my refuge and my fortress,
my God, in whom I trust."

Surely, he will save you
from the fowler's snare
and from the deadly pestilence.
He will cover you with his feathers,
and under his wings you will find refuge;
His faithfulness will be your shield and rampart.
You will not fear the terror of night,
nor the arrow that flies by day,
nor the pestilence that stalks in the darkness,
nor the plague that destroys at midday.
A thousand may fall at your side,
ten thousand at your right hand,
but it will not come near you.
You will only observe with your eyes
and see the punishment of the wicked.

If you say, "The Lord is my refuge,"
and you make the Most High your dwelling,
no harm will overtake you,
no disaster will come near your tent.
For he will command his angels concerning you
to guard you in all your ways;
they will lift you up in their hands,
so that you will not strike your foot against a stone.

Contents

Acknowledgements | viii

Introduction | 1

PART ONE: THE FIRST THREE STEPS: ISLAM, IMAN, INTENTION

Islam: Step One | 19

Iman: Step Two | 38

Niyyah: Step Three | 52

PART TWO: MORALITY AND THE FOURTH STEP

Morality and the Fourth Step | 61

Chapter Four: Morality | 69

Chapter Five: Listening and Speaking | 84

Chapter Six: A Few Words on Sex | 91

Chapter Seven: The Fifth Step | 101

PART THREE: STEPS SIX THROUGH NINE AND REFINEMENT OF CHARACTER

Chapter Eight: Steps Six and Seven | 109

Chapter Nine: Steps Eight and Nine | 117

Part Four: The Steps of Ongoing Maintenance

    Chapter Ten: Setbacks and Relapse | 127

    Ihsan: Step Eleven | 131

    Chapter Twelve: SERVICE: Step Twelve | 143

    Conclusion | 148

Bibliography | 153

Acknowledgements

First, I must thank my parents for their dedication to my recovery. Over the years, they have been my most loyal friends and staunchest allies, and suffered the most, more than me, as a result of my illnesses.

I especially want to thank my son for his patience with how distracted my work has kept me over the years, and for inspiring me to be a better person.

I would also like to thank Dr. Kim Norman who helped me bring this book to completion back in 2002 in the form of *It's All in the Mindfulness*, and his inspiration to do the work in mental health and addiction that I do today.

My sponsors over the years, Sarah McClure and Donna Peeples, also deserve to be acknowledged for all they have taught me, along with all the women in recovery who have patiently loved and persevered with me and with our community.

I would like to especially acknowledge Marin Lodge, where I first really got my feet on the ground with my mental health. Tracy and Vicky, you both loved me in spite of how difficult I was and it made a huge difference.

I need to thank my therapists who have taught me so much over the years, especially Dr. Sue Fleckles with her support of my writing and art, as well as Karen Sprinkels who has made such a difference in my ability to be creative and successful in my endeavors with her gifted use of EMDR.

Additionally, Larkin Street Youth Services, where I have taught mindfulness over the years, especially the youth, for their faith in me, and support for my work, as well as all the clients I have had over the years who have taught me so much, from how to clean my house better, to how to be a better and more mindful human being, including my early work teaching

Acknowledgements

mindfulness through Walden House at the Latino Commission, Project 90, and other places where I began to understand teaching mindfulness in practice as a smoking cessation instructor.

I need to also acknowledge Mr. Shames, my creative writing teacher in high school who was the first person to teach me to meditate.

The dharma teachers who have inspired me deserve special thanks as well, His Holiness the Dalai Lama, Jack Kornfield, Guy Armstrong, Philip Moffitt, Pema Chodron, Chogyam Trungpa, and all the many amazing dharma teachers who have taught me about mindfulness.

I wrote this book as a part of a senior project at Dominican University, and it is necessary to thank Father Bob Haberman for having faith in me that this work was worth doing, as well as the other teachers at Dominican who encouraged me to develop my understanding, including Scott Sinclair, Dr. Boitano, and Phil Novak.

Over the years I lost the electronic copy of the document and I thank Dr. Cynthia Andrzejczyk for transcribing it again, as well as her help as an editor.

Additionally, there are many teachers who I have studied with over the years from College of Marin, the Graduate Theological Union, UC Berkeley Extension, and CSU East Bay, who have made it possible for me to write, think, and understand these issues. A few people who deserve special thanks are Leah Shelleda, Ted Greer, Janet Mackintosh, Dr. Munir Jiwa, Dr. Ibrahim Farajaje, Bhante Seelawimala, and Dr. Rose Wong.

My gratitude as well to my reiki teachers whose instruction and guidance supported my efforts to bring this project to completion, Meg Siddeswari Sullivan and Tamara Nakhjavani.

Somebody who deserves my gratitude as well, Dr. Imhotep Ishmael Al Basiel, whose friendship and support have helped me many times over the last nearly twenty years.

I also want to thank my wonderful teacher Imam Mehdi Khorasani who I studied with for over a decade, as well as Dr. Robert Frager, Imam Zaid Shakur and Ustadha Saliha Shakur, Shayk Yassir Chadly, Dr. Rania Awad, Sr. Afaf Awaad, Sr. Rumana Abdullah, and all the countless Muslims who have taught me about the *diin* with their unconditional love and friendship.

Of the Muslim community I would also like to particularly thank those who have supported my writing, especially Sr. Amani, Sr. Manal. Sr. Azmia, Mama Maysoon, and the whole Muslim girl clique, as well as Dr. Hamada Hamid, Dr. Farha Abbasi, and Mary Firdausi from the Institute for Muslim Mental Health for their faith in me and their support.

I also want to thank all the magical and spiritual beings, fairies, angels, Buddhas, *Bodhisattvas,* saints, and ascended masters, family and friends, who have sustained me in my work over the years. This surely would not have been possible without you.

TRANSLATIONS

Quranic citations are taken from Muhammad Asad's *The Message of the Quran* (The Book Foundation, 2003) in the form of (Quran chapter #: verse#)

Sayings of the Prophet (PBUH) are taken from www.hadithcollection.com unless otherwise noted in the text.

TRANSLITERATION

Transliteration is used for Arabic words, and all words are italicized except for terms which are so common as to be part of the English language such as the Quran or Islam.

ABBREVIATIONS

(PBUH) Peace be upon him. All mentions of Prophet Muhammad's name are followed by this abbreviation in the Islamic tradition of sending peace and blessings on the Prophet when he is mentioned in writing.

Introduction

Bismillah Ar-Rahman Ir-Rahim.
In the Name of the Most Gracious, Most Benevolent.

THE SPIRITUAL NATURE OF ADDICTION

What do most addicts have in common? Many of them talk about feeling different, about feeling like they were not a part of anything, like they were somehow outsiders, peering into the world through a thick glass window pane while everyone else was inside, participating naturally. This feeling of being different is a common denominator for many addicts. Most addicts also used differently than others—they used more, they used longer, they used as if their sanity itself depended on it. Often, for many, it did. This feeling of being different was accompanied by feeling lost, as if addicts had been sent out into the world without a guide book that everyone else had received. They used the analogy of feeling rudderless, like they were the only ships on the sea, unable to steer the right course. Finally, there was an overwhelming feeling of emptiness. These types of feelings, while understood as chemical imbalances, are often symptoms of a spiritual problem. Happily, there is a solution.

First, we have to understand that as addicts, we often operate on the assumption that if we can just get the right drug, the right person, place, car, clothes, paycheck, orgasm, date, drink, or smoke, we will no longer have the sense of feeling adrift. The problem with this approach is that it constantly requires more of what we are taking to feel okay, and eventually, whatever we are using to 'fix' our feelings stop working.

In the course of this quest for wholeness and connection, we become totally self-centered. We are so obsessed with fixing the emptiness we feel inside that we gradually forget about everyone, and everything, around us. We think less and less about the feelings and needs of others because we are spending more and more time filling that hole inside ourselves, with whatever we are using. Eventually, some of us reach a point where we cannot even take care of the most basic needs such as eating, sleeping, and keeping ourselves clean because we are so busy staying high. Most addicts are deeply spiritual people who have gotten lost along the way.

The fundamental problem with the idea that more of something will fix the feeling of being different, or fix the problems that addicts have with life, is that this attitude is based on a misunderstanding of the root of the dis-ease felt by the addict. Once the cycle of addiction has begun, it will never be satisfied by more of the same. The solution, first and foremost, must be to stop using and apply something to heal the awful emptiness that remains. This healing is often achieved through working the Twelve Steps.

Mental illness and addiction share many commonalities. They are both chronic, are based in the mind and emotions, with an associated chemical component. Mental illness and addiction are illnesses which alienate the sufferer from the majority of society. Mental illness can range in severity and type from minor depression to bipolar disorder to severe schizophrenia, often accompanied by drug addiction.

When I was diagnosed with drug addiction, schizoaffective disorder, borderline personality disorder, serious depression and Post Traumatic Stress Disorder in 1994, I had very little hope. I dropped out of college and was suicidal. I was locked up three times during the summer of 1994, and under a 72 hour because I was a danger to myself.

The only rope that I could hold onto at the time was my faith, and my devoted parents. I couldn't write my full name on a form in the doctor's office because I was so sick. My parents thought that they had lost me for good. With the exception of a few incredibly loyal friends, I was utterly alone. I refused to take my medication because I had begun to attend Twelve Step meetings and couldn't differentiate between drugs and medication. I refused treatment and rapidly became sicker. In December of 1994, I underwent psychological testing and was informed that I could probably benefit from long term hospitalization. I flunked out of junior college, and in despair, agreed to commit myself to a live-in psychiatric facility. I spent six months living there, and another nine months in day treatment. I still left care long before they were prepared to let me go, as I was determined to go back to school and get my degree.

Introduction

Following several relapses, dropping out of school again, and returning one more time, I finally succeeded in transferring from junior college to a four-year college. I had been in therapy on and off for five years at that point, and continued recovery. I applied to graduate school and was accepted. Now, twenty-five years later, I have not used a drug in 23+ years and have not had a drink in 25 years. I have fully recovered from PTSD, have learned that I never had borderline personality disorder, and no longer suffer from symptoms of depression. I have worked all Twelve Steps and taken meetings into homeless shelters, juvenile halls, and mental hospitals. I believe that all this is possible because of my spiritual connection and the miracle that my Higher Power has worked in my life. I have a long way to go, but I continue to work towards higher levels of healing and recovery.

I made the decision that I needed to pass on my experiences because throughout my recovery from addiction and mental illness, I have been plagued by doctors who have been condescending about my spirituality when I am referring to my recovery from mental illness. I first wrote this book back in 2002, when this problem was far more pronounced. Over the last twenty years, there have been huge advances in the way the medical profession frames spirituality and recovery. However, there are still challenges. This is extremely important to address because for many people who are mentally ill, there is a spiritual component to their mental condition. Often, people hear and see angels, experience the Divine intensely, and have a variety of visionary experiences.

Many people believe that the mentally ill in our society have been the shamans, the *sadhus*, the people who in ancient societies would have been encouraged to travel into alternative realities. Unfortunately, those who do not dwell entirely in the physical world often suffer intensely in our society. In addition to being marginalized for a condition which is not necessarily even pathological, they are discouraged from seeking spiritual solutions to their problems because of the predominant Western medical approach to illness. This approach pathologizes all mental states which are different from the norm and, for the most part, spirituality as a whole. If doctors do not pathologize spirituality, they usually ignore this factor in a client's life.

The roots of pathologizing spirituality lie in the work of Sigmund Freud. It is useful here to compare the perspective of Freud with that of Ken Wilbur, a well-known Buddhist philosopher, on psychology to see how differently people view mental illness, and the related role of spirituality. Freud was the product of a medical establishment that sought to cure diseases by dealing with the manifested symptoms, and thus, he advocated talk therapy as a 'fix it' approach to get people functioning normally. Freud saw mental difference as an improper gear working in the mind that could be talked into functioning in a way that would allow the individual to participate in society again.

For Freud, religion was not part of the solution; it was part of the problem, and he described religion as "a universal obsessional neurosis." For Freud, all religious life was pathological. In his *Future of an Illusion*, he discusses extensively the falsity of religious ideas:

> Let us return once more to the question of religious doctrines. We can now repeat that all of them are illusions and insusceptible of proof. No one can be compelled to think them true to believe in them. Some of them are so improbable, so incompatible with everything we have laboriously discovered about the reality of the world that we may compare them—if we pay proper regard to the psychological differences—to delusions. Scientific knowledge is the only road which can lead us to a knowledge of reality of Ourselves.[1]

In *The Question of a Weltanschauung*, Freud continues his argument against religion, "Of the three powers which may dispute the basic position of science, religion alone is to be taken seriously as an enemy."[2] Freud then concludes, "Our best hope for the future is that intellect—the scientific spirit, reason—may in the process of time establish a dictatorship in the mental life of man."[3] Freud concludes this work by saying:

> [Scientific] work lays a rule like a sculptor at his clay model, who tirelessly alters his rough sketch, adds to it and takes away from it, till he has arrived at what he feels is a satisfactory resemblance to the object he sees or imagines. Besides in the older and more mature sciences there is even today a solid ground work which is only modified and improved but no longer demolished. Things are not looking so bad in the business of science.
>
> And what finally is the aim of these passionate arrangements of science? In spite of its present incompleteness and of the difficulties attaching to it remains indispensable to us and nothing can take its place. It is capable of undreamed of improvements

1. Freud, *The Freud Reader*, 705.
2. Freud, *The Freud Reader*, 785.
3. Freud, *The Freud Reader*, 790.

while the religious [mindset] is not. This is completeness in all essential respects. If it was a mistake, it must remain one forever. No belittlement of science can in any way alter the fact that it is attempting to take account of our dependence on the real external world, while religion is an illusion and it derives its strength from its readiness to fill in with our instinctual wishful impulses.[4]

Freud, is of course, the "Father of psychoanalysis." His biases against religion have been passed down directly through the years to our present day. The psychiatric establishment often tries to treat mental illness solely as a chemical imbalance in the brain, a narrow approach which eliminates the whole person from the recovery process. This attitude, combined with the derogatory clinical language, pathologizes spirituality itself among the mentally ill. Words such as "religiosity" are still used to refer to the intensely personal and spiritual experiences of mentally different persons. The psychiatric establishment sometimes prefers to believe that mental health can be discussed in "scientific" terms, and for a long time, for much of the psychiatric establishment, the scientific approach went hand in hand with a lack of tolerance for, or understanding of, the spiritual elements of humanity.

The attitude that we see Freud displaying in the above quotations is not an uncommon one among psychiatric professionals who we encounter along the way, and, in part, it is not entirely the fault of those professionals who display such an attitude. The training of most psychiatric personnel is based on the groundwork that Freud established. The huge advances in our understanding of the molecular biology of mental illness have served to bolster the approach to mental difference. Thus, religion is still seen sometimes as an enemy to be routed rather than an ally to be nurtured.

It is illuminating to think about the fact that Freud's understanding of science is totally outdated. He believed that science reported on an external world that the observer could study from an unbiased standpoint, the scientific belief of his day. This understanding of the possibility of objectivity has been totally destroyed by advances in nuclear physics. We now know that it is impossible to study the physical world without altering it.

Ken Wilber is a modern thinker who approaches mental states from a different point of view. For Wilber, mental states lie on a spectrum, sort of like the spectrum of microwave radiation to infrared or visible light. Each type of mental state, Wilber believes, is a different band of consciousness.

---

4. Freud, *The Freud Reader*, 791.

For Wilber, the Western scientific understanding of mental life—reflected by thinkers like Freud or people who limit mental difference to the scope of molecular biology—is entirely too limited, and basically incorrect. Wilber believes that religious life is a band of consciousness on the spectrum of human experience. As Wilber states in *The Marriage of Sense and Soul*, all elements are reflections of the "Great Nest of Being."[5] For Wilber, this nest has three levels: "the gross level (matter and body), the subtle level (mind and soul), and the causal level (spirit)."[6] He reiterates, "Physics studies matter. Biology studies vital bodies. Psychology and philosophy address the mind. Theology studies the soul and the relation to God, and mysticism studies the formless God-head or pure Emptiness, the radical experience of Spirit beyond even God and the soul."[7] He mentions that until the arrival of modernity, characterized by scientific materialism, and the reduction of reality to the gross level, this Chain of Being was taken for granted. Then came the scientific revolution. As Wilber states:

> In place of the levels of being was 'a flat land' conception of the universe as composed basically of matter (or matter/energy), and this material universe, including material bodies and material brains, could best be studied by science and science alone. Thus, in the place of the Great Chain of Being reaching from matter to God, there was now matter, period. And so, it came to pass that the world view known as scientific materialism became, in whole or part, the dominant official philosophy of the Modern West. [8]

Elaborating on this point a bit further, Wilber says that "according to scientific materialism, the Great Nest of matter, body, mind, soul, and spirit could be thoroughly and rudely reduced to systems of matter alone; and matter—whether in the material brain or material process systems—would account for all of reality, without remainder."[9] This mentality is exhibited in its fullness in the above comments of Freud, and still today, in parts of the medical community.

In *Spectrum of Consciousness*, Ken Wilber discusses his approach to mental health using the Great Chain of Being, and the spectrum of human

5. Wilber, *Marriage of Sense and Soul*, 8.

6. Wilber, *Marriage of Sense and Soul*, 9.

7. Wilber, *Marriage of Sense and Soul*, 10.

8. Wilber, *Marriage of Sense and Soul*, 10.

9. Wilber, *Marriage of Sense and Soul*, 13.

experiences.[10] Ken Wilber believes that mental states reflect many levels of the Great Chain of Being. Thus, for Wilber, mental states are multilayered and include spirit and soul. This view contrasts with Freud who tried to "scientize" the work of psychoanalysis in an attempt to make it acceptable as a scientific discipline to the people of his era. To this day, psychiatrists are M.Ds., i.e., doctors who deal with mental differences as a physical problem that can be fixed by medicine, not a spiritual problem at all. Many people try to limit mental difference to the level of matter alone. Therefore, for those of us who feel that we are experiencing an existential crisis rather than a pathological religiosity, it is useful to look at Wilber's perspective on psychology.

An approach that deals with all levels of the Great Nest of Being is the Twelve Step program. The Twelve Steps address the spiritual nature of the pathological behavior of drug addiction. The Twelve Steps deal with the layers of mind, soul, and spirit through an approach which is centered on walking a spiritual path in response to a problem which is seen as having manifestations at all levels of the Great Chain of Being. The physical level is addressed at the level of physical compulsion to use drugs. The mental level is the obsessive thoughts related to getting high and getting more drugs, or more of whatever feeds the addiction. The spiritual is seen as being expressed through self-centeredness and the lack of connection to God-head, or the spiritual source of the individual.

There are also other programs which address substance use. These other programs sometimes use religion, sometimes not, but they also include emphasis on self-control and self-reflection in the interest of developing better habits that produce a happier life. Some of these programs are SMART Recovery and Life Ring. Behavior modification approaches have been systematized in a variety of ways. However, there is a significant amount of research that if you do have a spiritual path that you follow, utilizing this path in the process of recovery is effective and helpful. This has been scientifically studied in Christianity, Islam, Buddhism, Judaism, and a variety of other traditions as well as the very loose interpretations formed by the millions who have found their own answers through the Twelve Steps themselves. For those of us who are mentally ill, it is possible to apply the principles of the Twelve Steps simultaneously to our addiction and to our mental differences through physical action, medication, mental action, therapy, and spiritual action, through prayer, meditation, and a spiritual

10. Wilber, *Spectrum of Consciousness.*

path. The interrelated levels of the Great Nest of Being all come together in our recovery from mental illness and drug addiction, if we choose to apply the Twelve Steps.

One of the potential problems of discussing spiritual approaches to mental difference is the demonization of the medical approach to mental illness. This problem is aptly described in Wilber's *Spectrum of Consciousness* where he discusses those caught up in dualistic mindsets. In dualistic oppositions, which we have engaged in for 2,500 years, since the time of Greek philosophy, it has been,

> . . . almost as if man were given two pictures of his body—one taken from the front, and the other taken from the back. In trying to decide which of these views was 'really real,' man divided into two camps: the Frontists, who firmly believed that only the picture taken from the front was real; and the Backists, who steadfastly insisted just the opposite. The problem was a tricky one, for each camp had to devise a theory to explain the existence of the other, so the Frontists had just as much trouble explaining the existence of the back as the Backists had in explaining the existence of the front. To avoid the contradiction, the Frontists spent their time running away from their backs, and the Backists were just as ingenious in devising ways to run away from their fronts. Occasionally the two would cross paths, yell obscenities at one another, and this was called philosophy.[11]

It would be easy to become immersed in a discussion of why the medical model is so inadequate, and thus fall into the trap that so many of us have been stuck in for so long of being afraid of medicine, therapy, and the medical establishment in general as a source of possible help for our difficulties. To attack the medical establishment is not the point of this text. In fact, medical approaches can be critical parts of addressing mental illness and addiction. Instead, I would like to critique some of the inadequacies and shortcomings of medical models that exclude the realms of soul and spirit in hopes of better understanding their approaches. By doing so, this text might be able to highlight a different approach, that of a spiritual path.

11. Wilber, *Spectrum of Consciousness*, 27.

SPIRITUALLY INTEGRATED APPROACHES TO PSYCHOLOGY

This text does not assume that all people are unable to see the relevance of spirituality to mental difference, and it is important to note the huge advances that *have* been made in the field of psychoanalysis regarding the approach to religious belief since Freud founded the talking cure back in the late 19th century. Even in the early 1900s, Freud's most famous disciple, Carl Jung, gave a great deal of attention to the issue of religion, and the pervasive character of religious symbolism in his discussion of the collective unconscious, and in his works on religion and psychotherapy specifically. Jung recognized the importance of spirituality for society. He says of Eastern religion, "But if the white man does not succeed in destroying his own race with his brilliant inventions, he will eventually have to settle down to a desperately serious course for self-education."[12] This course of self-education that Jung refers to is Eastern Philosophy. At the same time, Jung did not believe that Eastern philosophy should be taught to people with mental difference, or even to the average person. He was still reluctant to endorse Eastern philosophy, as a whole. Following in the footsteps of Jung, many therapists and analysts have explored Buddhism, specifically as a way to empower their ability to do therapy. The body of literature which explores the complementarity of psychoanalysis, recovery from addiction and mental illness, and spirituality is constantly growing. Even so, there remains some hostility and degradation of the experiences of people who are in the grip of mental differences which make functioning in society difficult.

Following Jung, there were developments in the integration of spirituality with psychology and psychiatry. This work progressed in Muslim circles in large part among Sufis in the West. The theories of Sufi psychology built on Jung, as well as other thinkers, and began to theorize psychological approaches that took the idea of the soul and spirit seriously. Early work on this was predominantly done among Sufis in the West, and then recently over the last ten to twenty years there has been a burgeoning Islamic psychology movement.

This is of course referring to the modern era. Historically, mental health was a huge priority in the Muslim world, with the first mental hospital being built by Muslims centuries before Europeans even thought about

---

12. Jung, *Basic Writings*, 100.

psychology. However, in the modern world the renewal of this tradition is a current work among mental health professionals who are reviving the Islamic science of mental health and psychology. Yet, in the modern West, this work has been happening for a long time among Sufis, and is only starting over the last twenty years to really hit mainstream Muslim culture.

SUFISM

At this point. it is important to define what I mean by Sufism and Sufis. There are many people who do discount the word Sufism as illegitimate, but for me, my teacher was clear: while we were Muslim, we were also Sufis. He was part of the International Sufism Organization, and involved with Sufi groups that were modern and inclusive although his personal training was more traditional.

Sufism has been defined by those who take it as a serious and legitimate movement within Islam in a variety of ways. The main way that I use the word Is In relation to the Sufi understanding that the religious life involves seeking to come closer to the Divine through self-understanding and self-knowledge. While I became acquainted with Sufism by looking up my teacher in the phone book in the late 1990s in response to a comparative religions class at junior college, I already believed in the basic tenets, and that is why it has always been my path to me. The idea of mysticism, self-knowledge as knowledge of the Divine is a Christian idea, a Buddhist idea, and a basic logic to all mysticism. That is why Sufism is known to many as the mystical branch of Islam, or simply as Islamic spirituality.

Part of the reason that much of the work in Islam and psychology has been done by Sufi scholars is that the path of Sufism within the Islamic tradition is focused on goals which are also traditional goals of Western psychology. The development and refinement of the self, greater self-understanding, and insight are all core parts of the traditional work of Sufism. The idea that developing the self is a core part of the spiritual life is defined by an understanding of the self, discussed in parts two and three of this book, that emphasizes a division of the self that is very different from Western psychology and puts spirit, soul, and heart at the center of the understanding of the true nature of the human person, what is known as the ontology of the self in psychology. Ontic means real, and logos means science, or logic, and ontology if therefore the understanding of the real fundamental nature of something. When applied to people, ontology means what is the core reality of the self, i.e., what does it mean to be human, and who are we really?

The ontology of the self that is recently being more developed by mainstream Muslim thinkers, a broad and far reaching and rapidly growing movement, was first developed and discussed in the modern world by Sufis. However, the ideas of self-development go far back into the Islamic tradition, and many people work extensively with the ideas of the famous Islamic scholar Imam Al Ghazali, who is well known not only as a Sufi himself, but as making Sufism an acceptable part of orthodox Islam.[13] The ideas of Sufism that both medieval and modern thinkers discuss in their writings are a perfect fit with the twelve steps. The holistic approach of the steps, the spiritual emphasis, and the emphasis on self-control, self-knowledge, and self-purification comprise, in many ways, the core disciplines of Sufism, as well as the major teachings of most modern Muslim scholars, harkening back in part to the teachings of Al Ghazali on the spiritual path, the Islamic path, and the Sufi way of life.

Many people have been able to use the path of Islam to lead them into recovery and out of drug addiction. There are some who have used an Islamic approach to the Twelve Steps. However, the Twelve Steps as a spiritual path offer an approach which is spiritual but not specifically tailored in general to the needs of those of us who have extreme mental difficulties. Islam and the Twelve Steps as approaches to co-occurring disorders provide answers, but there is a paucity of literature on the way that the two paths can complement each other in overcoming addiction and mental illness. I cannot name all the people who I have seen fail to achieve recovery due to their inability to handle having co-occurring disorders. The prognosis for people in recovery who have both mental illness and addiction is much worse. It's much harder to handle both problems than one or the other. There are many people who have died due to this inability to deal with schizophrenia or depression. It is not an exaggeration to say that learning better ways to deal with co-occurring disorders is a matter of life and death for some. This topic is more than a philosophical exercise.

Perhaps this text will add to the body of literature available for those of us diagnosed, rather than those of us for diagnosing in a way that creates more of an opportunity for people to heal themselves. Regardless, I have decided to put together a few thoughts based on my experiences in dealing with addiction and mental difference through spiritual practice in the hope

13. Davis, "Sufism from its Origins to Al-Ghazzali," 241-256.

that the process that I have undergone while healing myself can help others, especially through mindfulness, and connection to the Divine, what Paul Tillich called the Ground of Being.[14]

The following text reflects a variety of spiritual traditions and their relationship to recovery from addiction and to recovery from mental illness. The purpose of including so many spiritual traditions is to show that any and all traditions can be applied to the steps of recovery. Although I have personally chosen one specific tradition, that of Islam, and within Islam, Sufism, I believe that applying a variety of spiritual traditions is the key to recovery rather than any one religion in particular. The unity of all major world religions is a basic belief of Sufis. Sheik Muzaffer Ozak, of the Jerrahi Sufi Order said:

> Sufism is not different from the mysticism of all religions. Mysticism comes from Adam (God's peace upon him). It has assumed many different shapes and forms over many centuries, for example the mysticism of Jesus (God's peace upon him), of monks, of hermits, and of Muhammad (God's peace and blessing upon him). A river passes through many countries and each claims it for its own. But there is only one river.[15]

The concept that all the prophets, Buddha, Moses, Jesus, and Muhammad, peace be upon them all, were describing the same Truth, the same Light, the same Source of Being, is a basic belief of Sufism.[16] The Quran teaches that if God had wanted us all to be one faith, we would be already. The diversity of religious traditions is one of the gifts of the diversity of our humanity as a whole.

MINDFULNESS

This text focuses on mindfulness which is a thread that runs through all religions, while exploring a variety of perspectives, including Buddhism, Judaism, Christianity, Islam, Hinduism, paganism, and science. The reason for this is that to apply spiritual principles, we need to be present. The concept of mindfulness as presence is a connection that some people have written about from a Sufi perspective. This focuses mindfulness in a way

14. Tillich, *Ground of Being.*
15. Ozak, *Love is the Wine,* 1.
16. Barks and Green, *Illuminated Prayer,* 7.

that is actually more applicable to recovery because it takes mindfulness far beyond breathing and into the realm of a spiritual practice of deepening connection and awareness in every way possible in life as a goal of life.

One question is mindfulness of what, and why (personal communication, Dr. Robert Frager, 2019). Is mindfulness just a practice to improve focus, health, and emotional states? In fact, mindfulness has been shown to be an effective tool to recover from addiction on a scientific level.[17] Mindfulness based relapse prevention in particular has become a well-researched and developed intervention for the treatment of addiction and has a manual that has been developed for use by recovering individuals.[18] Mindfulness has been researched as an Islamic intervention in therapy and mental health as well.[19] Mindfulness has been scientifically shown to improve all sorts of health outcomes. But this is not the end point for mindfulness from a Sufi perspective, nor arguably is it the endpoint from a Buddhist perspective.

The point of presence, and mindfulness, from a Sufi perspective is to develop a connection to, and understanding of, Ultimate Reality in order to live life more fully, in love and truth. If you are trying to find a location with a map, and the map lacks sufficient detail you might find your goal, but you will be challenged to do so. If living in truth and love, in harmony with the Divine, with True Being, is the goal, at least we should be starting with the intention to draw a map with the actual end location that we desire being clearly marked.

There is a famous saying which, regardless of its authenticity, has been the basis for Sufi reflection for centuries. The saying is that God said, "I was a hidden treasure and I desired to be known, so I created the creation that they might know me." This saying can be found in a wide range of Sufi writing, and many teachers quote it, including Rumi and others, although authoritative hadith collections do not include it,[20] and many deny its validity. This hidden treasure that is God is the "present," the treasure in all life and living, the present worth loving, the gift of the Divine that pervades all

17. Witkiewitz, Greenfield, and Bowen, "Mindfulness-Based Relapse Prevention with Racial and Ethnic Minority Women," 2821-2824.

18. Witkiewitz, Greenfield, and Bowen, "Mindfulness-Based Relapse Prevention with Racial and Ethnic Minority Women," 2821-2824.

19. Isgandarova, "Muraqaba as a Mindfulness-based Therapy in Islamic Psychotherapy," 1146-1160.

20. www.hadithcollection.com which is the source for the majority of the hadith in this book does not include this saying.

being. God, according to Sufi understanding, is Omnipresent, and creation is nothing but a series of veils over that reality. Mindfulness, then, for some Muslims, is basically the ongoing remembrance, awareness, and tuning into this underlying Truth. Mediation is one source of tuning in, as are prayer, being in nature, contemplation, and other avenues of spiritual awareness, many of which are mentioned in this book.

In the sense that this book is about presence, this book is about spirituality not religion. Partly this is because it is action-based despite its comments on religion. At this point, we might ask what is the difference between spirituality and religion? My definition of the difference is that spirituality is always action based, while religion can remain merely a theory. Religion can be spiritual, but it is not always so. What kind of action is spiritual action? Any action which helps and does not cause harm. Based on whether or not something is helpful and does not cause harm, one can say whether or not an action is spiritual. I must emphasize again that spirituality is about action. The dogmas of religion often do not lead to action, and that is why they are often derided as useless, and insofar as they lead us to avoid the world and the problems of our lives, they are.

The difference can be explained concretely in terms of the idea of murder. Not to kill is one of the Ten Commandments, and one of the Buddhist precepts. It is crucial to every world religion. But the mere idea of not murdering has not always stopped people from killing, just because they go to church and hear the idea. Not killing becomes spiritual when you get rid of your guns and become a vegetarian. Thus this text is spiritual when it talks so much about religion, partly because at the end of each section, there is a meditation on mindfulness. What is mindfulness? Being fully present, being in the now with compassion and without judgement. Mindfulness is necessary for any spiritual action because all action happens in the now. It is also necessary to healing, and to the practice of the Twelve Steps.

When I wrote this book originally in 2002, I stopped there. I stated, "This book is about spirituality not religion." However, bowing to the liberal peer pressure that religion is a dirty word is also highly problematic. So, I'd like to say this book is also about religion. It is about the universal religion that involves acting in accordance with Divine Laws that are revealed in all the great world religions. It is about love. My teacher, Imam Mehdi Khorasani taught that Islam, and Sufism, can be summed up in one word: love. The Dalai Lama, the leader of the Tibetan people, who was friends with Imam Khorasani, is famous for saying, "My religion is kindness." The question of mindfulness of what and why can be partly answered that for Sufis, it is loving awareness of the present moment, loving awareness of the Divine, and loving awareness of life. Mindfulness is about loving the present moment, loving presence, as Kabir Helminski's book says, *Living Presence.*[21] This is the perennial truth at the heart of all religions, and is systematized throughout human history in organized religion.

Who or what is the God of this Divine Law, this Primordial Religion? A woman in recovery once said to me that the Eleventh Step is the only step which can be worked out of order. The Eleventh Step states, "We sought through prayer and meditation to improve our conscious contact with the God of our understanding praying only for knowledge of his will for us in the power to carry it out." It is never too soon in recovery to start to become mindful and live in love in the present moment, learning to follow one's truth and highest understanding of the Divine. In Twelve Step groups, it is accepted that one of the key phrases of the Eleventh Step is, "God as we understood Him." There are endless variations among all the Twelve step programs members on what this understanding looks like. People from all religious traditions, and many with no religious tradition at all, who have a personalized "Higher Power," work the Twelve Steps. To some extent this is reflected in this text which covers many traditions. There is no need to follow any specific understanding of what God is to work the Steps. As some people say, "You can use the doorknob if you want; just pick something." For many, it is found in the natural world. One person I know used to call her God "George." This text incorporates a variety of world traditions, but the concrete applications and exercises are based on mindfulness, a universal spiritual principle, and this principle's incorporation into a life of mental wellness, drug-free, in harmony with Divine Law.

Living in presence is not merely about being aware and non-judgmental though. It is not an exercise in concentration, although that matters. Mindfulness is about living compassionately with love for ourselves and those around us. Someone has said that the opposite of addiction is not abstinence but connection. The idea that to be in recovery we need a loving connection to other people and our community is based on the idea that to recover from the isolation of addiction, we need to develop the skills needed to connect with love to others, and to ourselves.

Mindfulness, in the sense of loving the present moment then, is a minute to minute, day by day practice of caring about ourselves and those

21. Helminski, *Living Presence.*

15

around us. While I am not a super great meditator, I do have a strong moral sense of love and connection, and this has been built through the practices and approaches outlined in this book. All of the mindfulness exercises are practices that I incorporate into my daily life. I believe there are those among us who will far surpass me in being able to apply these principles very rapidly. I look forward to learning more as together, we learn how to be more spiritually based, more mindful, more present, more loving, and together, healthier. May this be of benefit.

PART ONE

The First Three Steps: Islam, Iman, Intention

Islam: Step One

Step One prayer: There is no reality except Reality.
La ilaha il Allah.

WHAT IS THE RELIGION of Sufism? Fundamentally, it is Islam. What is Islam? It is surrender, submission, to Ultimate Reality. In essence, that is the First Step. Step One states, "We admitted we were powerless over our addiction and our lives had become unmanageable."[1] The first step in recovery is this admission that we cannot use drugs successfully. Likewise, the first step in recovery from mental differences is the admission that we have some difference which makes it difficult for us to live in the world. The First Step is a combination of surrender to Reality, and commitment to embark on the spiritual path. It is hard to imagine a person who would know that there is an ultimate truth that would give a person happiness and peace and not try to come closer to it. That is the first pillar of Islam, the *Shahada*, or the testament of faith, the acceptance of Islam. Anyone can take this step. However, no one said that the religion of Islam, or recovery, or the spiritual path are always easy, although they all can be. The spiritual path is often easier than any other path we could take, both in the short term, the long term, and the eternal sense.

1. You can locate more about the traditional interpretations, as well as the source of the wording of the steps in both the Basic Text of Narcotics Anonymous (Narcotics Anonymous World Service, *Narcotics Anonymous*) as well as the Big Book of AA (Alcoholics Anonymous World Service, *Alcoholics Anonymous*). Due to the nature of anonymity, as well as many other reasons, I do not claim to represent or speak for any Twelve Step fellowship at all, however several are mentioned in this book.

Sometimes, it is very difficult to accept reality, and for those of us with co-occurring disorders, a diagnosis of mental difference and addiction. Either we wanted to think that we were like everyone else, or we didn't want to admit that we had anything wrong with us. Accepting diagnosis is difficult. At the same time, accepting that we are different can be tremendously liberating. It is the beginning of a new perspective. So that's why everything was so difficult!

How does rehabilitation begin? It begins with realizing that there is a challenge to face, and it means coming to terms with that challenge, usually in the form of accepting a diagnosis. Unfortunately, many people with mental illness are misdiagnosed. General ignorance and sometimes outright racism can influence doctors in charge of diagnosing illness and prescribing medication.

For example, in the Surgeon General's report in 2001, African Americans were three times as likely to be diagnosed with schizophrenia, versus bipolar disorder, than any other ethnic group.[2] It is well documented that there is an equal proportional occurrence of schizophrenia among all racial and ethnic groups. This kind of criminal mistake can be very damaging. Bipolar disorder in the manic stage and severe schizophrenic psychosis are indistinguishable in displayed symptoms. Schizophrenia, however, has a much lower recovery rate than bipolar disorder (at least when bipolar disorder is properly diagnosed and treated). We must question our doctors to see if our diagnosis has been tainted by their bias.

Additionally, African Americans are generally prescribed 2 to 3 times the amount of medication that other groups are prescribed, in spite of the fact that at least one-third of African-Americans metabolize medication much more slowly than any other group due to a specific, non-pathological liver function. Thus, African-Americans often need lower rather than higher doses of medication. This overmedicating can prevent the mentally different from even being able to think clearly enough to address the crisis, or general situation, that they face at the time of diagnosis.[3]

In light of the dangers of misdiagnosis and the difficulties some of us face based on race and ethnicity, it is important to be careful whom we trust in our treatment. Doctors are often quick to prescribe medication without taking the time to follow up, and seeing psychiatrists can be so

2. Office of the Surgeon General (US), *Mental Health: Culture, Race, and Ethnicity*

3. I thank Dr. Kim Norman for alerting me to these disturbing revelations from the Surgeon General.

traumatizing that the mentally ill avoid it at all costs. Many of us have seen too many doctors, taken too many pills, and are just tired of the routine. It is beneficial to have a friend or family member advocate for you if you are in that situation.

Mental illness often makes it so that we don't have to face reality. Whether we are escaping into psychosis, or avoiding life through depression, or totally not caring about life because of mania, we avoid the fundamental nature of life. We run away. Misdiagnosis makes dealing with the problem worse, so we should be careful about accepting a diagnosis too readily.

DIAGNOSIS

So how do you know if your diagnosis is right? Well, diagnosis is designed to direct the treatment medically. For one thing, it changes the medicines you should take depending on the problem with your brain chemistry. But what you need to know is that diagnosis is designed in the best-case scenario to give you more control over your situation. It can be a source of ease, being able to actually name, "Oh, I have depression" or "Wow, I have Bi-polar disorder."

Not confusing the label with the person when talking about substance use and mental illness is really important. There is often a tendency for people to say, "She's depressed" or even "She's Bi-polar." This equates the person with the disease. This attitude is completely wrong. A person has depression; she is not herself the depression. Or a person has a mental illness, and the person themselves are not summed up and defined by their diagnosis or their mental states. They might be mothers, fathers, sons, daughters, friends, partners, workers, artists, musicians, but their existence is not that they are "mentally ill." In fact, I try to use the words "mental health challenge," or my preferred description, "mentally different," whenever possible.

Words are magic to some extent. In *The Four Agreements* Don Carlos Ruiz talks about this.[4] We put spells on each other and our reality with our words. This can be a good thing, when we say things like, "I know I can figure this out," and it can be a bad thing when we say things like "This is impossible" or "This is hopeless." Never say that. There is always hope!

---

4. Don Carlos Ruiz, *Four Agreements*, 25–46.

INTRODUCTION TO A FEW BUDDHIST PRINCIPLES

On one level, mental illnesses are just extreme expressions of the spectrum of consciousness that have gotten in the way of living a productive and satisfying life. But if we look at the great spiritual teachers, they all seem to point to the fact that struggling with life is a part of the plan. It is the nature of life. There are a lot of people who say, "Oh, there's no tests" but then there's the rest of us who are convinced, there really are tests, in fact, to some extent, life is filled with tests. The Quran is clear that believers will be tested. (Quran 29:2) What does this have to do with mental illnesses? Well, it relates to the part where we start to get oriented to how to get better, and to the topic of presence, and mindfulness.

The Buddha's First Noble Truth was the first thing he uttered when he attained enlightenment under the Bodhi Tree. What was it? Well, within the limits of translation: Life is Suffering. When the Buddha attained enlightenment, he applied the method of the doctors of his time to the problem of human suffering. The doctors of his day first identified the cause of an illness. Then they ascertained whether or not there was a cure. Then, if it was possible, they came up with a cure, and they applied the cure. The Buddha diagnosed the problem of life as suffering, and the cause of that suffering is craving, or thirst, thirst for more of whatever would solve the suffering of life.

For the mentally different and those of us who have problems with always wanting more of whatever we are addicted to, the alcohol, drugs, or food to name a few, we, likewise, have to identify the problem. Often our problem is that we are suffering. Life isn't working anymore. That's why we ended up in rehab, or a mental institution. Our diagnosis is just a label that someone has put on our suffering. The doctors of our day have identified their words for what to call our dis-ease. So, what is this suffering really? As we have said, for the Buddha, the disease of humanity is suffering, *dukkha* in Pali. All human beings, said the Buddha, suffer. Suffering is a natural part of life. In fact, suffering is the nature of life. You don't have to be an addict or mentally different to suffer, said Buddha. It's universal.

Suffering, said the Buddha, is caused by craving. We can see a similarity here to addiction. Craving is the nature and source of addiction. When we are suffering from the onset of addiction, we feel craving. This craving, said the Buddha, is common to all people; those who are addicts have responded to this craving by using drugs, and that has made the craving far worse.

The Buddha said there was a solution to craving. He believed that suffering could end, and he suggested a spiritual solution. Likewise, the Twelve Steps suggest that freedom from addiction is possible, and they offer a spiritual solution. The Sufi path, the Christian path, the Jewish Path, the Hindu path, the Pagan path, all propose various solutions to the problem of suffering. Buddhism has much to say about suffering, and the nature of suffering, and much of it is unnecessary to repeat here. The most important thing to understand about the Buddha's diagnosis of suffering was that he believed it is based on a fundamental misunderstanding. While most people think the self is very solid, the Buddha concluded that they are wrong. The Buddha said that the self is not solid. If we look at the body, we cannot say where the self is located. If we say it is in any one part of the body, what if that part is gone? What if the body atrophies and the mind remains active? But if we say it is in the mind, what of the body? Or what of the emotions?

The Buddha taught that the self is not solid. The Buddha said a chariot can't be identified to be just one part; likewise, self is made up of many parts. To speak further on this point from a modern perspective, the car isn't just the tire or the engine. It isn't just the seats or the speedometer. It's everything together, parts that make up the whole. Each part of the car is made up of the sum of its parts. The engine is made of metal and plastic, and now, computer chips. Who made these? Where did they come from? The car is not only made up of the parts, the parts are made up of parts. To offer another analogy, when does your cup of coffee become your body? And when does this air we breathe become hemoglobin, and what does that have to do with the self? You get my point.

Ignorance about the self causes suffering and makes us think we can do the impossible. We try to hold onto the self, but it doesn't really exist! The self is by nature, what Buddhism calls, "empty of own being," the doctrine of emptiness.[5] It doesn't have an existence in and of itself. So, when we try to protect it and keep the outside world from affecting it, we are going to be very disappointed. The self isn't real, and it's impossible to separate it from the outside world.

---

5. For more information on the Buddhist concepts and ideas covered in this book, you can refer to Phil Novak and Huston Smith, *Buddhism: A Concise Introduction*. I studied Buddhism in undergraduate and graduate school as well as Buddhist centers around San Francisco, and the concepts covered in the book are common knowledge from a multitude of sources.

PHYSICS AND INTERCONNECTEDNESS

For the scientist who doubts my introduction of the Buddhist understanding of the self, let me comment on modern physics. Modern physics has discovered that at the most fundamental level, we are basically amorphous waves of probability. The quark is the smallest building block that physicists have isolated, and it behaves in a most unusual way. When quarks are measured to see if they are waves, they behave like waves. When they're measured to see if they are particles, they behave like particles. When you measure their location, you aren't able to measure their velocity and vice versa. When you send them in opposite directions (they come in pairs), they spin into directions until you measure one of them at which point they decide simultaneously which will spin in which direction and spin in opposite directions from each other instantly, no matter how many trillions of light years apart they are. Thus, they do not operate the way that our reality operates. They defy reason. They are not waves, but they can act like waves when we look for them to be waves. They are not particles, but they can act like particles when we look for them to be particles. They are like water and air at the same time! That they can communicate with each other instantly seems to defy any logic within reason.

All matter is made up of these particles, and they exist just as a kind of soup that only differentiates itself to us because we are bound by time, which they are not. In other words, we are fundamentally made up of a weird vibrating fog of energy that just happens to look the way it does to us. Why do quarks operate the way that they do? The physicists haven't figured it out—they are still working on it. They have even determined that the soup that makes up who we are isn't separate from the soup that makes up the chair that I'm sitting on or the moon or the Crab Nebula. So, the Buddha was onto something.

Now, modern medicine is caught up in a Newtonian model of the self. When Newton discovered the laws of motion and gravity, many people thought of the universe as a giant clock. Everything operated based on simple laws which could be reduced to simple mathematical equations. People thought everything was determined by the way motion and gravity operated. They thought that the entire universe operated simply: if you drop a ball of lead, expect it to fall to the ground: everything was believed to be operating like little balls of lead moving around, determining not only where the planets would go next, but how the entire course of human events would occur. This reduction of the world to Newton's laws of science became known as scientific materialism. The universe was thought to be like a machine, mechanistic.

Modern medicine thinks that the human body operates like a machine. Put in a pill, press that lever, sit clients on the couch for 50 minutes, if it's affordable for them, and they will start working properly again. Modern medicine tends to treat the brain like a complicated machine that just needs the right oil change to get it to work normally. Unfortunately, this understanding of the brain is based on a deterministic picture of the world in which everything is understood to operate under rational principles, but the quark soup described by modern physics feels no compunction to operate based on what you and I understand to be reasonable, and we are made of that same quark soup.

Thus, the self is not solid just as the Buddha stated. We think it is, but in reality, it is mostly space, made up of this vibrating fog of energy, and it is inseparably connected to the rest of the universe. However, the mechanistic model of the self says the self is solid. It starts at the feet and ends at the head. But the real self isn't solid; it's just pieces of things which seem connected.

There is a growing body of analysts who agree with the idea that therapy can become more informed and more effective through using Eastern religion, especially Buddhism, because they recognize the mechanistic model that Freud aspired to is outdated. They recognize that the self has many layers of being, just as Ken Wilber says it does. Some analysts want to work towards a more holistic model which incorporates spirituality. Psychology, of all medicinal disciplines, should be prepared to integrate spirituality because the spirit is without a doubt a part of the self, and part of the mind. And when addiction is involved, a spiritual solution is perhaps the only approach which will accomplish the vast adjustments necessary for total recovery.

THERE IS NO BEING BUT BEING

This concept that the self as the mundane mind perceives it is actually an illusion is present in the Abrahamic faiths; in fact, it is a central tenet. Now some people will disagree with this, but it is a very well-established tradition, and it appears clearly in the scriptures, the Torah, the Bible, and the Quran. Islam's declaration of faith is "There is no god but God." This has been stated by many to mean there is no being but Being, or there is no reality but Reality. Understanding reality in these terms is a principal perspective of Sufism. This concept is also present in the Torah in the words of God in the book of Exodus in the Old Testament when God says to Moses to tell the Israelites, "I AM has sent me to you." (Exodus 3:14) The concept is also present in the New Testament both in the words of Jesus, who said, "Before Abraham was born, I AM." (John 8:58) and also in the letters of Paul who stated repeatedly that God is in all and through all, and Christ is in all and through all.

The concept that there is an underlying unity which is appearing as multiplicity to our limited human minds is a central tenet of all of the major world religions. Sufis believe that this world is similar to a veil, or infinite veils, covering over the true underlying Being of God. As Shayk Muzaffer wrote, "We are all Divine. We belong to God. We are neither the before or the after. We are a part of truth. When that is forgotten, when that remembrance is erased from our heads, then we are in danger."[6] The Divine is the underlying unity, and we are merely expressions of this, momentarily appearing like waves in the sea. So this understanding of the self as an illusion is not exclusive to Buddhism. As my teacher, Imam Khorasani wrote, "This expanded world is nothing but a manifestation of God's will. All the creation known and enjoyed by us, all spiritual position, physical matter, and intellectual forms are points from the Intention of the Great Creator."[7]

BACK TO THE SELF-MISTAKE

Okay, so the Buddha said that the problem with most people is that they feel that they have a very solid self. They believe that the self is one piece, and it belongs to them and, "Gosh dammit I'm going to take care of it and make it feel good and it's mine not yours, and I want it to last as long as possible." But this is not possible. First of all, the self is inevitably going to get sick and die. Suffering. And the self is never satisfied. It always needs more food, more water, more air, and in the case of an active addict, more drugs. Suffering. Not only is the self not going to stop suffering through feeding itself, it isn't even separate from the world, so it is constantly being upset by death, sickness, and outside phenomenon which it can't control, and it's constantly changing. Because change is constant, the more we try to hold on to self, the more upset we become.

6. Ozak, *Love is the Wine*, 32.

7. Khorasani, *Way of Success and Happiness*, 12.

For addicts, this obsession with self is even more pronounced. Addicts, more than other people perhaps, are born aware of how transient their self is. Carl Jung called addicts "frustrated mystics." We instinctively know that we are not solid, and that produces a fundamental uneasiness or fear. Many people talk about fear, self-centered fear, being the core of the disease of addiction. Addicts can't accept this changing self they live in and just go about life as business as usual. Like the Buddha, addicts recognize the self is not solid, but unlike the Buddha, addicts often don't know the cure, and if they do, they don't know how to apply it effectively. They feel how unsteady the world is and they're terrified, and in their fear, they try to tune out. They turned to drugs as a way out. The uneasiness felt by addicts that they don't know how to navigate could come from the fact that addicts have seen the non-solidity of the self, but everyone else seems to be convinced of its permanence. So, addicts feel like, "Wow, why does everyone else seem to get it when I don't?" The ironic part is addicts were right when they felt, intuitively, that things just weren't quite as neat and tidy as the world seemed to portray. We were onto something.

When we found drugs, we discovered a way to control the way that we felt. We no longer had to wonder if we were going to be happy or sad, or be afraid of change, because we had something that didn't change—the high. The problem was that eventually, as we needed more and more, the high turned from fun, to fun and trouble, and then only to trouble. Then we didn't know how to escape. We rejected the rules of society, but we were still stuck in the society that we had rejected, and life became really unmanageable.

If we accept that we are just as the Buddha said, that the self cannot be isolated, and, as physics says, that we are merely vibrating possibilities on our most fundamental level, we can see that there is no separation between me and you. Whatever I do to you to make you happy, I do to myself. When I hurt you, I hurt myself. There is no separation. When I reject society, I reject myself, because we just can't remove ourselves from the rest of the world. An example of this is that we can reject the rule not to steal, but if we do steal, and get caught, we are stuck going to jail.

At this point, it is useful to comment on the Golden Rule. There is the old saying that we should "do unto others as we would have done unto us." Ultimately, there is no separation between self and others, and this makes infinite sense, because when we are doing unto others, we are actually doing unto ourselves! This leads us to another old saying, "What goes around comes around." Unfortunately, we make the self-mistake, and we think that we should only take care of ourselves. So, we do things which are unethical such as lying, cheating, killing, and hurting others in all kinds of ways. We think we can get away with it. But we can't. There's no escape. Mental illness similarly removes us from the world. Through psychosis, mania, and depression, we fixate emotionally and escape from the world. Reentering reality can be very difficult because we have to experience the uncertainty of change.

ACCEPTANCE

When we accept our diagnosis, we admit that something is wrong with our way of being. In the mechanistic model, the approach was to try to fix things by working on the self as if it were a machine and by hitting a lever to make it work properly. In the model of interconnectedness in the Great Chain of Being, we can recognize that we don't just have a chemical problem, we also have an existential problem.

In both mental illness and recovery from drug addiction, acceptance is a key factor in rehabilitation. Before anything constructive can be done to approach the problem, the addict and a person with mental difference must accept the world as it is and the challenge of facing it without either the drugs or the dysfunctional cognitive, emotional, or mental functions. Without this acceptance, treatment, therapy, medication, and self-help groups are of no avail. Honest acceptance of the problem in the intrinsic 'yuckiness' of life and suffering has to replace denial if recovery is to be possible.

In mental illness and addiction, the problem of denial, of running away from life, gets even worse for most of us. We are running away from running away! When we are in denial, we tell ourselves that we don't have a problem, despite all the evidence to the contrary. We tell ourselves that we will deal with life later, that we will deal with it if we can just sleep 10 more minutes, or get high one last time. That is why the first step is so crucial and has to be so thorough. We have to accept on a deep level that we have to face everything and recover (the first letters form FEAR) and not forget everything and run (another four words whose first letters form the word FEAR). If we believe the diagnosis of mental illness and drug addiction to be correct, then we have to work to accept the realities that it brings.

This part of consciousness is where the admission of powerlessness in the First Step is so crucial. With addiction, the First Step is all about overcoming the desire to run away. It's a lot easier if you understand that there just isn't any escaping. No matter how fast you run, or how far you go, you are always connected to everything. We are all powerless over our connectedness to the universe; no matter how many drugs we take, we are going to remain connected. In fact, the thing that you were trying so hard to protect, your self, can't be protected at all, and you have to accept that too. You cannot run from the Divine Reality, because at your essence it is you. That realization can be tremendously painful.

Sometimes for the mentally different, the problem changes. When we are suffering from mental illness, we can have a hard time communicating, and we feel the separation between ourselves and others even more intensely. At this point, understanding the underlying reality of the problem is so important. We can reconnect to the universe, our hearts, and our fellow travelers on the planet, by contemplating this fundamental unity, and through the First Step, in surrendering to the basic nature of the unity of all things.

Now, most of us have been running away for quite a while. We haven't been dealing with the rest of the world that we live in; we have only been thinking about how to get high. This means that we haven't been addressing a part of the world, which infringes on our world, no matter how much we want to remain isolated. But because we are all connected, it is sure to catch up with us at some point. The attempt to deny the world that we live in, and our connection to it, produces a fundamental chaos in our day-to-day realities because how can we cope with something we are not even acknowledging as having a right to affect us? The First Step says not only are we connected to the world, but in attempting to deny the world we are connected to, our lives become very chaotic. The surrender to our place in the holistic universe involves both the acknowledgment that we are connected and can't run away, and that we have to address the world we live in in some fashion for our lives to work.

Suffering is the nature of life, said the Buddha. Because of the suffering that many of us have experienced, we want to deny the world we live in. But at some point, that just becomes impossible. When the world infringes forcibly on our consciousness through increasing levels of unmanageability, we can begin the process of change by waking up to the unity of all things.

SERENITY AND ACCEPTANCE

The concept that facing reality is the starting place for recovery is really important. It is reassuring to think that the First Step is about surrendering to reality, about not fighting anymore. Continuing to try to deny the truth leads to a lot of problems. Accepting reality creates a lot of serenity because it just is. It's a question of mindfulness and presence: reality just is, and just to be aware, to be conscious. To some extent, the use of drugs is an attempt to remain unconscious. Whether people are jacking up their systems to accelerate towards the subtler planes of life, or just trying to avoid their feelings, a degree of trying to escape life is inherent both in drug use and mental health challenges. Just being willing to accept life as it is, to face your feelings, can be a starting place that cuts out a lot of chatter and leads to a lot of serenity.

Judeo-Christian-Islamic traditions have always taught that all things are God's will, and there has been a huge emphasis on predestination in different moments in Western religions. Just as God says, "I AM," life is what it is. This has interesting connections to what we know about space and time. How can God be all knowing? Where is free will in this? I certainly don't claim to have the answers to all these questions, but I can offer my insights. One is that we are bound by time in ways that are not absolutely true in all places in the world. Due to the connection between space and time, time has completely stopped in black holes. If there is a Creator, obviously this Creator would be beyond the reach of time for both reason and by virtue of having created time itself. So, if everything has already happened, laid out like a scroll to the Creator, it could lead one to be accepting that this is written down already; it's God's will, destiny, kismet. It's a plan. For Sufis in particular this belief is the foundation for a radical acceptance of life as it happens. This acceptance of all things that happen as God's plan also supports the commitment to being patient in the face of adversity. As one woman said to me, "There is a plan and the plan is good." This basic Sufi belief is a good starting place for the Second Step, but I'm getting ahead of myself.

The belief in a power greater than ourselves can be reinforced by all the times we have seen things work out. And when things don't work out the way we want or plan, there is always the comfort that life itself is a precious gift. There was no guarantee that this beautiful earth would come into existence, with nature, trees, oceans, and all the beauty of the world. It's a gift, and just our existence is something to be grateful for. The Sufi saying goes, a believer can be content in all situations. In good times, believers are grateful, and in difficult times they are patient. This is the fundamental surrender of the First Step. Just let go and let God.

THE FIRST TRADITION

The First Tradition says, "Our common welfare should come first, personal recovery depends on NA, GA, OA, any A, unity." We can see how the statements of the First Step and the First Tradition relate if we see the First Step as a time to reflect on the holistic nature of the universe, and our powerlessness over that fact. If we want to recover from a dual diagnosis, we need to stop running away from everything and surrender to life as it is. In doing so, we break through our denial and begin to look for solutions. The First Tradition teaches us that we go through this process in unity with the rest of the beings who are on the planet, as one force, with a unified purpose. Because we are all connected, if I merely look after my own little world, I can't really make much progress. I need to become a part of the greater whole, and stop living the lie that I can live separate from everything around me. In uniting with the movement of so many beings toward a more spiritual life, and getting out of the way with my own little egotistical agendas, I strengthen my own health and that of those around me. We have to do it together. We have no choice.

THE LIFE OF BUDDHA

Before we start discussing the first step and Buddhism and launch into practicing mindfulness, we should look at who the Buddha was, and how he worked his first step, because it was the key to his attaining enlightenment. The story of how the Buddha came to be enlightened can be a source of inspiration and guidance for us as addicts and mentally different.

The Buddha was the son of a great Indian king. After he was born, his father, the king, called together astrologers and wise men to tell him what his son's life would be like. They said that the Buddha would either be a very great king or a very great spiritual leader. The king wanted his son to follow in his footsteps, so he tried to protect his son from anything that would send him on the spiritual path. The Buddha lived in palaces surrounded by young, beautiful women. He always had enough food and the finest clothes. He never saw anyone old or sick or dead. Whenever he went out of the palaces, his father would clear the streets of all beggars and sick people—all the people who were suffering so that the Buddha would not know that suffering existed. One time, when he was out on his chariot, the Buddha saw an old man, a sick man, and a dead man because his father had not cleared the streets up quite well enough. When he realized the nature of human existence, he left his life in the palace and went to the forest seeking a solution to human suffering.

After many years following a variety of spiritual paths, he finally gave up and sat down under a tree and said he would not move until he attained enlightenment. The demon Mara came and tempted him all night long, but the Buddha held his seat. There is a famous *mudra*, or hand gesture, which is depicted on the night of the Buddha's enlightenment. While he was sitting under the Bodhi tree, and Mara was tempting him, the Buddha reached out his hand and touched the ground. The Buddha said with this gesture, "I have a right to be right where I am, and no matter what you do I am not moving. I understand life is suffering, and you can make me suffer more or less, but I am staying right here regardless." When dawn came, the Buddha had realized the truths of the universe and had become enlightened. He went on to teach the religion that became known as Buddhism for the rest of his life.

By analogy, as addicts, we are at varying stages in our spiritual walks. Some of us are trying to stay in the proverbial castle and deny any sickness, death, or suffering. Some of us are out in the forest, and instead of trying to keep working towards enlightenment, we have gotten sidetracked and are hanging out in the treetops loaded. Some of us are convinced that if we get a good enough 'nod' going, we will be able to sit under the Bodhi tree long enough to reach our enlightenment. And some of us have gone out and actively recruited disciples for the religion of no-suffering through constant intoxication.

I would like to suggest the admission of powerlessness and unmanageability, and the first step is to sit down under our own personal Bodhi trees and touch the ground. We can surrender to the fundamental nature of suffering, and from there work towards liberating ourselves from the chains that have bound us to drugs, mental illness, and spiritual sickness of all types. No matter how much craving or fear or denial we are in, we must choose to accept reality and the suffering it brings without succumbing to the temptations of Mara, or to the illusion of seeking something outside of ourselves to cure our suffering, and our desire to attain liberation from it regardless of how hard it gets. When we are tempted again to use drugs, or to run from the world in the cloud of mental turmoil, we can simply touch the ground and hold our seat, surrendering to life as it is.

POWERLESSNESS AND EMPOWERMENT

The idea of surrendering to reality as it is, and the concept that we are powerless can be really scary. A lot of people criticize the idea of powerlessness in the Twelve Steps as validating a lot of the negative messages that they have received in life. There are several responses to this. One is that the admission of powerlessness in the First Step is about aligning ourselves with reality, more than admitting we have no choices. It's not, I am powerless, I can't decide anything. The thought is, I can't decide to deny reality, and there are things that I have to accept that I have at times in my life unsuccessfully tried to fight against.

Additionally, this reality that we have fought against can be really overwhelming. Feelings can be painful. Life can be difficult. However, the First Step does not work by itself in a vacuum. The First Step is immediately followed by Steps Two and Three.

Finally, if in fact we want to stop at the First Step, it is really the only step that we have to really get to stay off drugs, because one of the core truths of this step for addicts is that we are powerless over our addiction, over using people, places, and things, outside of ourselves to try to deny reality as it is. If we simply step up to life and face it, deal with it, accept it head on with all its good and bad parts, and stop running from it, that is the First Step, and that is the core of recovery. It is a tremendously empowering decision to face life on life's terms. We can all do it. As the saying goes, our feelings can't kill us. However, what we do with them can hurt us if we try to avoid them.

Reservations are places in our hearts and minds where we have decided to hold out the hope that we can successfully deny reality. Maybe, if the pain gets to be too much, we could stop working on ourselves, or find a way to work on ourselves that involves fixing our problems with something other than an honest engagement with life as it is. Reservations are the places where we have already decided certain roadblocks are going to necessitate leaving the path, or turning around to follow old ways of being.

Reservations usually lead to some sort of relapse. However, relapse is often just a wake-up call that the attempt to deny reality is inevitably unsuccessful. The beautiful thing about reservations and relapse is that recovery is always available if you want it. You may have to swallow your pride and humble yourself if you've told everyone that you are never going to use again and you show up as a pack a day smoker, completely psychotic, and with a face that's picked to shreds. But if we can reassert our decision to accept life on life's terms and face life we can survive and recommit to the path. A way to avoid this is to really assess our reservations and try to overcome them before they overcome us.

One way to do this is to identify as a person in recovery. Many of us found an identity as addicts, we were dope-fiends, we wore pot leaves embroidered on every possible item of clothing, and our entire life was rooted in our identity as drug users. Or maybe we thought of ourselves as so awake and psychic, that we were completely telepathic, and medication was going to interfere with that. I recently woke up in the morning and thought my car had been stolen. I filed a police report, and then a few hours later realized I had walked home from the train station and left my car in the parking lot. I decided I needed more medication. It was difficult because I have an identity to some degree of being awake, and I was worried about falling asleep. However, my identity as a mother, a daughter, and a social worker were far more important, so I doubled my medication. An identity which I have taken refuge in as an addict is being straight-edge. My identity as a person who doesn't use drugs gives me an additional defense. It is something to consider.

There is no reality but Reality. Surrendering to this truth is the straight path. Surrender means not running towards a high, not pulling the covers over our heads and refusing to get out of bed, not raging when someone doesn't act the way we want them to, but being present with life, being mindful, with love, peace, compassion, acceptance, and honesty. That actually is a very powerful place to be, but how do we do that when some of us may have never learned the necessary skills? That is the journey of the spiritual path, and of the steps.

BALANCE AS THE GOAL

There is danger in pursuing mindfulness or spirituality like a drug or a fix. Spirituality can be an escape route. This is why mindfulness is such a powerful tool in recovery. Our efforts, according to Sufism, should lead to a balanced life. The Buddhist Path is described as the Middle Way. Similarly, the Islamic path is described as a middle path, neither extremely oriented towards denying oneself or indulging oneself, but about living an awakened, balanced life.

THE MIRACLE AND MESSAGE OF THE PROPHET OF ISLAM (PBUH)

Many people in recovery have heard of the analogy of the life of the Buddha, and the awakening of the Buddha to recovery. Less well known is the analogy to the story of Prophet Muhammad (PBUH). However, there is a clear analogy that we can apply.

When the Prophet (PBUH) was about 40 years old, he was married, and in the habit of taking time to retreat to a cave to meditate. One night, he was in the cave and a voice came to him, a voice from the Archangel Gabriel, that said "Read" or "'Iqra" in Arabic. Being the most honest person who ever lived, and being illiterate, he responded that he could not read. Gabriel, or Gibreel in Arabic, then picked him up and squeezed him saying again, "Read." The Prophet (PBUH) again said he could not. He thought his bones would break. He was so scared that he was shaking. A third time the angel squeezed him and said "Read." The Prophet (PBUH), afraid, returned to his wife in the middle of the night, trembling, afraid he had lost his mind. When he told his wife what had happened, after wrapping him in a blanket. She said to him that he was not crazy but that the voice was from God. This was the beginning of the revelation of what Muslims know to be the greatest miracle of the Prophet (PBUH), the revelation of the Holy Quran, a mercy and guidance to all creation. This famous night is known as the Night of Power, and Muslims celebrate it every year in remembrance of the beginning of the revelation of our Holy Book.

How does this relate to the First Step? You might see where I am heading with this. We are often gripped at what is known as our bottom, when all seems lost, by a force that squeezes us and tells us to wake up, and live a different way. When we live this new way of life, when we accept this call, as you must have to be reading this book, we have the opportunity to bring a message to others with our life. As some say, the Prophet (PBUH) was the walking Quran. We are given the opportunity to be the message of recovery and to have the blessing of the miracle of recovery in our lives. While we certainly will not transform the whole world the way the Prophet (PBUH) did, we can transform the suffering of those around us with a message of a better way of life. If we have reached our bottom, where things have gotten intolerably bad, and it has destroyed our families, and our friends, we have the opportunity to answer the call of recovery, surrender to the miracle, and bring the light of hope to our loved ones.

I am not saying we will be prophets, just as no one has ever said that taking the First Step is exactly the same as the enlightenment of the Buddha. But I think the analogy is valid, that we need to listen to the call of a higher path and commit to carrying a message of a better way of life. We can do it, even if it is just for ourselves, knowing that certainly we will benefit others in the process. This miracle of recovery, this message of freedom from mental illness and addiction, is perhaps the greatest miracle we can offer to the world. We have a responsibility to work for it, and that can be done through the Twelve Steps.

MINDFULNESS AND STEP ONE

We are just beginning to practice the Buddhist principle of mindfulness when we realize the truths of our lives, the truths of the non-solidity of the self and the truth of suffering. Noticing reality is something which is the first best step in becoming mindful. Noticing the opportunity we have to carry a message and be walking, breathing miracles is a gift that we can give ourselves and those we love.

FOCUSING ON CRAVINGS

The next time you have a craving, take your hand and touch the ground with your finger. Tell yourself you'll sit right where you are until it passes. The temptations of life don't have power over you if you know you have a choice, a choice to not pick up. And as the saying goes, "If you don't pick up, you won't get loaded." If it gets really bad, just keep your finger on the ground. Usually, it takes two hands to do whatever you need to do to get high!

Part of quitting is often trying to survive cravings without getting high. When a craving comes, you can pay attention to it, and just notice it. What does it feel like? Where is it in your body? What is your mind saying to you? Often just the act of paying attention to cravings is enough to get through them. Often people react to cravings in a split second, when they have the option to stop and just be present with the craving. It may be more than you can do to resist, and that is part of the process of getting clean for some people. If it is too overwhelming to resist cravings through attention, self-talk, and other tools, sometimes it is a really good idea to go to detox, or to treatment.

MINDFULNESS AND DIAGNOSIS

Next time you have a feeling related to your mental difference, whether it is the desire not to get out of bed, the extreme mood fluctuations of being bipolar, or the intense distractions with schizophrenia, come back to your body and just feel exactly where you are. Tune into your breath. Notice yourself in a chair or on your bed. Try for a few minutes as you lie in bed at night to breathe carefully and stay with your breath. Then take note of how you're feeling. Do a mini check-in with yourself on where you are emotionally and mentally, just as you would in a group. Learn what it is like to be you, however you are, without judgment. If it helps to label it as your diagnosis, do so. If it helps you to just name the feeling, you can do that too. You can love, accept, and embrace the present with the gentle awareness of your attention.

MINDFULNESS, AND THE NON-SOLIDITY OF THE SELF

One way to discover the non-solidity of the self is to think and to be present with interconnectedness. When you are eating, as you chew your food, you can be present and think of all the elements that have gone into the food that is now becoming a part of you. When you breathe, think of all the trees that turn the carbon dioxide into the oxygen you need. And when you want to use, think about all the things which connect to you that will be harmed by you hurting yourself. As you become more conscious of the interconnectedness of life, your ego gradually loses its tremendous hold on you. You realize that things just aren't as much about your isolated trips anymore. There's a whole big world out there that you can't help but be a part of just by breathing and eating. This can be tremendously reassuring and satisfying because we aren't bound by our little worlds quite as much. We can find peace within our place in the gigantic universe that we call home.

Iman: Step Two

Step Two prayer: Guide us, and increase us in guidance,
and make us a reason for guidance.[1]

IMAN AND STEP TWO

Faith is a central part of life. We all have faith in something. In Islam the
word for faith is *iman*. While Islam is the first step of the religion, and
makes you a Muslim, *iman* is the second step of the religion and makes you
a *mumin*, or a believer. The concept that being a believer is a higher level
than simply just being a Muslim is an incentive to progress from simple
acceptance of reality to the decision to live in accordance to the dictates of
that reality. Faith is the essence of spirituality. It is characterized by action.
This action is the day-to-day substance of the spiritual path, but what is it
characterized by? Faith is the belief in a power greater than ourselves and
our limited trips, according to the Second Step, a power that can restore us
to sanity from the insanity of mental illness and addiction, and beginnings
of living by the belief. Faith is a dialectic, or a relationship and dialogue,
between thought and practice. It requires a clear idea about a Higher Power,
as well as concrete action to be in relationship to a Higher Power. As the
Bible says faith without works is dead. (James 2:17) Faith is a combination
of belief and action. So, the Second Step involves hammering out what we
believe, as well as beginning to apply this belief with a daily program of
recovery.

1. I learned this prayer by oral memorization, as well as other prayers in the book
in classes over the course of the last ten years with my Quran teacher Sr. Afaf Awad to
whom I owe much of my practice of Islam. They naturally became part of my spiritual
practice. However, it is possible to find some of them as well as many others in the excellent book by Mawlana Ashraf 'Ali Thanawi, *Accepted Whispers*.

GNOSTICISM

There are significant disagreements throughout history about who God is, who or what is a Higher Power. For example, Judeo-Christian-Islamic culture has long oriented itself towards a good God. Yet many people question this assumption. The ever-present suffering in our world leads many people to believe that the world is evil, and that the creator, if there was one, must be some sort of sadistic power tripper. These questions about whether or not God can be good, if God even exists, are not limited to our modern world.

At a certain point in my life, I became interested in an early Christian heresy called Gnosticism. Gnosticism was much in vogue when it was popularized by a number of Harvard professors and others of the academic elite. A great number of texts were unearthed in 1945 which gave us access to an understanding of Gnosticism which had been previously unavailable as the church fathers had systematically burned the majority of the Gnostic texts.

As I explored Gnosticism, I discovered something which I thought had great relevance for the modern world. Early Gnostics saw the world as fundamentally evil. Instead of seeing the creator as good, they saw him as ignorant at best and evil at worst. Most Gnostics believed that the God of the Old Testament was a lesser deity who had brought the world into being out of ignorance and that the world was inherently bad. The only cure to the evil of the world was to escape by turning to the true source of light, the God who predated the creator of the world.

So many people feel no hope for the world. Between the threat of global nuclear warfare, the progressive environmental degradation, the problems of overpopulation, misallocation of resources which has led to starvation, poverty and hopelessness for the majority of the planet, and the abuse of power by those in control, not to mention the current environment cultivating fear of terrorism, many people have despaired of the human species ever getting right with itself. Many people feel even God is evil when they look at the world, just as the Gnostics did 2000 years ago. How could a good God make a place like this?

For those of us who have been suffering from mental illness or addiction of any kind, the suffering has often been much more personal. We have lived on the streets, we have been hungry, and we have suffered abuse. We sometimes face these issues with clinical depression as well, so how do we pick up our heads? Is there any hope?

HOPE THROUGH SPIRITUALITY: FINDING SPIRITUAL ROOTS THROUGH THE SECOND STEP

The Second Step calls upon us to believe that at the very least, we can achieve personal recovery and freedom. When in the depths of the dual diseases of addiction and mental illness, sometimes it is hard to see any light, but the Second Step calls us to do just that. The Second Step states, "We came to believe that a power greater than ourselves could restore us to sanity." The Second Step is all about hope. It calls upon us to believe that we can transform our suffering through a Greater Power than ourselves. What is this Power that the Second Step talks about? For each person, finding this power takes personal effort. The Twelve Steps use the word God often. They have even referred to God as "Him" sometimes. But a major belief in all Twelve Step recovery programs is that this word can be interpreted any way that you want. There are atheists who work the steps!

In each of our lives, there are things which bring us peace, things which give us perspective on our little trips. I would like to refer to these powers as powers that bring us peace. It could be the ocean, or some other aspect of nature. It could be a specific tree or a traditional idea of deity. It could just be the people who were following spiritual paths. It could be other people in our lives who seem to have more perspective on things than we do. One power that can bring us peace is the simple act of being mindful. Often, our suffering involves worrying about the future or the past. It involves adding injury to insult, so to speak, by complicating the present moment with all the other things which are not actually present.

The Buddha said that all life was suffering, but he also said suffering can cease. If all life is suffering, then how can suffering cease? The Buddha suggested something which is known as the eightfold path. The eightfold path involves eight actions which can liberate us from our suffering. They are usually divided into three sections. The first two pieces of the eightfold path are what we talked about in Step One: knowing that the self-mistake is just that, a mistake. These factors are right view and right thought. In other words, it relieves a lot of our suffering just not to make the mistake of thinking that we are so solid, or that we are in any way isolated from the rest of the universe. This is the right view, and the right conception of the self and is connected to right thought.

The second part of the eightfold path involves living right, and I talk about this section extensively in part two. These factors are right speech, right action, and right livelihood.

40

The last three factors in the eightfold path involve purifying our minds. They are right effort, right mindfulness, and right concentration. In this text, I talk a lot about mindfulness. To practice mindfulness takes effort and concentration. These are the final pieces of the eightfold path, and are included in the mindfulness exercises at the end of each chapter. The great thing about the eightfold path is that it works no matter what your Higher Power is. You can practice the eightfold path if you are Buddhist, but also if you are Christian or Muslim. You can practice the eightfold path if you are a pagan or a witch. You can practice the eightfold path if you are an atheist. It doesn't matter. The Buddha said that the way to end personal suffering is through the personal spiritual practice of the eightfold path.

Through the course of this book, we will be focusing again and again on mindfulness, but in what context? That is the choice of each individual. For each of us in recovery from mental illness and addiction, finding what one's personal spiritual and religious values are and how to practice them takes a lot of work. In essence, Steps Two through Twelve are a path to finding one's own method of right mind, right living and right spirit, one's personal eightfold path. Step Two begins the process by asking us to come to believe that we have the ability to be restored to sanity through spiritual practice and by challenging us to begin the search for our own values about what our spiritual practice will look like.

Many of us come from traditions which we feel alienated from. Thich Nhat Hanh says,

> Many of our young people feel disoriented. They no longer believe in the tradition of their parents and grandparents and have not found anything else to replace them. Spiritual leaders need to address this very real issue, but most simply do not know what to do. They have not been able to transmit the deepest values of their traditions, perhaps because they themselves have not fully understood or experienced them. When the priest does not embody the living values of a tradition, he or she cannot transmit them to the next generation. You can only wear the outer garments and pass along the superficial forms. When living values are absent, rituals and dogmas are lifeless, rigid, and even oppressive. Combined with a lack of understanding of people's real needs and a general lack of tolerance, it is little wonder that young people feel alienated within these institutions. [2]

---

2. Hanh, *Living Buddha, Living Christ*, 88.

For me, I have always felt connected to the Judeo-Christian-Islamic tradition. At the same time, I am aware of the vast number of people who have been murdered in the name of the man who said do not kill, the enormous accumulations of wealth by Church officials following a man who died without a shekel to his name, and so forth ad infinitum.

It doesn't matter where you come from. You can find a way to live that works for you in the Twelve Steps because you get to choose to do it, however you want. All that matters is that you have an open mind, and hope. There are those of us who feel that there is no hope to recover from our mental challenges. We are so depressed that we cannot get out of bed to even take our medicine or go to therapy. We are so psychotic that we can't finish a thought about how to begin to recover. For these people, I have a suggestion: Sit down. Place your hands on your knees and your feet flat on the floor. Breathe in and breathe out. Now begin to listen to the sounds around you. Maybe there is a car going by, or a bird singing, or a breeze blowing. Maybe the room smells like a hospital, and the walls are painted that annoying blue color. Maybe you're hungry. Maybe you ate too much for lunch or breakfast or snack or dinner or whatever. If you sit still for a minute, you might find there was a fundamental rightness inherent in the present moment.

Within the present moment there is only now. As the old saying goes, "The past is gone, the future isn't here yet, and the present is a gift. That's why it's called the present." The Buddha taught that in the present moment, we can discover the non-solidity of the self, our subsequent interconnectedness to the world, and the resulting joy of living despite the suffering that comes along our path. When we are busy getting high, we are focused on how we're going to feel. Once we are high, we are usually unable to feel, or we are already focused on our next hit. We're so busy chasing around trying to avoid suffering that the present got lost. Mental illness is much the same way. We are so busy with our thoughts of how awful life is, or so manic, or so psychotic and caught up in hallucinations that the sound of a car going by or a bird singing is something we missed completely. For many of us, getting high might have started out fun, but soon it got ugly. At the end, we were isolated and terrified. The present, however, can be wonderfully fresh and new in early recovery, and if we allow it, the present can be the best medicine around. When we find the present moment, we can also begin to search our hearts and minds for the roots of our spirituality and our own spiritual path.

LEARNING HOW TO LIVE IN THE WORLD

For many people who have mental illness, there is already a strong connection to God. Unfortunately, there is a difficulty connecting to people. In the Western world, there is little space to go to monasteries, and most monasteries don't take crazy drug addicts off the streets as members, although a few do. But, for most of us who have strong connections to God through psychosis, we have been invalidated over and over. We feel like nobody understands us. We might see visions of Angels and hear the voice of the Divine, but doctors are telling us we are psychotic, and they just won't listen to reason.

My experience with this is that we have a choice. We can remain in our own little world and commune with God to our hearts content, if we want. We have that choice, but we are missing out on the world we share with other people. We are missing out on the present. Anyway, we've got the afterlife to trip out for eternity, if we are really that close to God. We might as well hang out with the other fleshly beings while they're around. Spirits don't give good hugs.

The Buddha recognized that altered states of mind existed, but he used them only when they had bearing on the process of the evolution of mindfulness and the movement toward enlightenment, or nirvana. In David J. Kalupahana's, *A History of Buddhist Philosophy*, Kalupahana mentions psychokinesis, clairaudience, telepathy, and clairvoyance among other high states of mind. For example, he states, "Telepathy, the ability to read the thought processes of other people, served as a useful means of understanding the intentions of his listeners and communicating with them in a more effective way."[3] When I was first diagnosed, I was convinced that I was telepathic. Unfortunately, no one else was convinced, especially when I went running off to meet people and places where they had told me in my head that they were going to be and didn't show up! In fact, I became a little skeptical after a while. But I continued to have experiences with people telling me information I would not have any knowledge of in any other way in my head, and it is subsequently confirmed in the unfolding of events.

Should I take medicine to reduce this unique manifestation of my mind? Well, I thought for a long time that medicine was the enemy of my mental prowess in the psychic realm. But after dwelling in space for a while, I realized that there was a lot going on in this world that I was having a hard

3. Kalupahana, *History of Buddhist Philosophy*, 40.

time tapping into, without the help of medicine. For example, I wanted to get my bachelor's degree, and I couldn't study without tripping out constantly. I couldn't concentrate on the printed page. I found that by taking medicine, I was able to pursue my education. I wondered, as well, when I first began to take prescription medication if it would hurt my creative process. I felt very inspired to write poetry and paint when I was off meds and heard a lot of uninterrupted psychic background music. But I found that taking medicine allowed me to focus my creative process and become even more creative than I had been before.

Psychiatrists are still working to improve the medicines used for what they call mental illness. It sometimes takes a while to find a combination that is effective. With the help of a good doctor and some perseverance, it is possible to enjoy a higher standard of life, and greater connectedness to the world we dwell in than would be otherwise impossible. Obviously, taking medicine is more complicated for those of us who have substance abuse issues: we are confronted with the difficulties of having to take mind altering chemicals in a program of complete abstinence. There are often people who do not understand. It is important not to judge those of us who choose to take medication to handle what we have been dealt.

However, altered states of mind can be a big distraction from the here and now. They can be a great way to escape from reality. I still find myself wandering off, and I probably will for the rest of my life. Some of us want to wander off permanently. For those of you who are ready to give up on the world and just off yourselves, why are you in such a hurry? You are going to die eventually anyway. Just hang out for a while. It's a lot less messy. As the saying goes: "Permanent solution, temporary problem."

The present moment is the perfect time to figure out the roots in our spiritual path. The Second Step doesn't have to happen quickly. The Buddha wandered around for years eating grains of rice until all his bones showed while he tried to figure out his path. Then one day, he just sat down under a tree, attained enlightenment, and started drinking bowls of milk. The Second Step is about a process. Processes take time, even for the Buddha.

SANITY AS SERENITY

Serenity, a lack of frenzy and chaos, is in some ways the essence of sanity. Being the best people we can be, and turning it over and letting other people be exactly who they are involves letting go of the illusion of control and accepting reality. Actual reality, where we make mistakes and learn from them, live in the moment and make rational decisions for how to be our personal best, is a source of finding peace. When we are in our addiction this is not the state we exist in, which is why we seek recovery in the first place. We aren't happy, we aren't serene, even if it's only our loved ones whose criticism has disturbed our high.

We all have different levels of addiction. For instance, when I obsess about money and how I am going to be able to make necessary changes in my life, I am actively feeding my addiction with chaos, frenzy, and uncertainty. When I choose to eat poorly, I am feeding my addiction with unrealistic expectations of making myself comfortable with food. Unwillingness feeds the negative and self-loathing aspects of my disease. These frenzied chaotic expressions of addiction can continue long after the drugs have long left our systems.

We see examples all the time of how being more open to others and making positive efforts to participate in life can transform our suffering and insanity to peace and serenity. Smiling more and being more approachable are a restoration to sanity from our social isolation, alienation, and difficulties in relationships.

BEING A BURDEN TO A LIFE OF SERVICE

Although the focus on service specifically comes later in the steps, the idea that sanity involves usefulness and service is a central idea of recovery. The essence of recovery is not just stopping drug use, or becoming able to hold a conversation, it is about living a productive, fulfilling, satisfying life. Leaving behind the insanity of selfishness, self-centeredness, and self-destruction is a central part of the sanity of recovery and the Second Step. When we begin to re-enter the world, and participate in Twelve Step meetings, we see people who are happy, peaceful, and useful, people whose lives are enriched and enlarged by their love and service to others. Part of the insanity of addiction is the isolation, dereliction, and depravity of living a life that harms us and society. Part of the process of recovery is believing we too can be productive, and of service.

I often think about the idea that we are special, and in fact we are. We know from chaos theory the old idea that a butterfly flapping its wings in China can cause a hurricane in the Pacific Ocean. Likewise, we can not isolate importance, or specialness, or power, or status to any one factor, individual and action. Each one of us, each blade of grass, each fallen leaf, each smile we share with a stranger or our family, the way we make our cup of tea, can save the world, can make all the difference in the future of all humanity. This idea is in the Quran in a variety of ways including the verse which says, "if anyone saves a life, it shall be as though he had saved the lives of all mankind." (Quran 5:32) Our actions are tremendously important. Picking ourselves up and committing to making every effort to contribute positively in whatever way we can is a restoration to sanity and begins with the simple day to day act of self-care, recovery, and not using drugs. Even the decision to try to recover, if it seems impossible to stop drug use, or take your medication today, even the intention to try to be positive and of service is a restoration to sanity.

This is epitomized in Twelve Steps by the emphasis on service and overcoming selfishness which characterizes addiction and mental illness. If it seems too much to do anything positive, just taking our medication, and not using drugs is something we can do for our loved ones that is tremendously of service. Being restored to sanity is a progressive upward cycle that we can begin with very small acts of willingness.

RESTORATION TO SANITY VS. CONVERSION TO NORMALCY

For those of us who are living with mental health challenges, being restored to sanity might not be something that we really want. Reentry can be somewhat of a shock. The Second Step for me will never stop. Stress and schizophrenia directly correlate. I also need to come back to my breath and try to have faith again. Depression can recur. Mental illness, like addiction, is chronic and cannot be cured; it can only be treated. The Second Step merely calls us to believe that we can get better at coping with life, not necessarily to want to be like everyone else. Sometimes I feel really special that I can see lights and hear voices. Sometimes I feel like it's a gift. Then, I need to have faith that I am who I am for a reason, just like everyone else, and learn to be present with who I am.

Being restored to sanity isn't about being really aggressive or about changing who we are fundamentally. A lot of doctors set out to change people from mentally different to mentally normal. The Second Step doesn't say we came to believe that we could become like everyone else. It says to come to believe that we could be restored to sanity. Sanity in the

Twelve Steps has a very specific definition. It means not repeating the same mistake expecting different results. If you miss therapy, and you don't tell your doctor, expect to be charged for an hour of nothing. If you do it again, expect to be charged again. If you miss your meds for two days and have a manic episode, wait six months and do it again, expect to have another manic episode. Sanity is not learning how to be like everyone else. In fact, I have received training at a psychic institute as a clairvoyant. They told me all the clairvoyants were schizophrenic. I know this might sound a little far out, but I want to learn to handle my mind as it is.

Seriously, the Second Step for a lot of mentally different people can be very threatening. It feels like an attack. Especially when we have been through so many doctors telling us that we have to change, now we feel like we are being told the same thing. However, the Second Step is about waking up to the fact that there is no escape from oneself and one's connectedness to the world. There is nowhere to run. And being sane means that we can just be ourselves in that moment, as crazy as we are, however we are. Being restored to sanity in the Second Step is learning how to work with insanity constructively.

Pema Chodron says, "You can feel like the world's most hopeless basket case, but that feeling is your wealth, not something to be thrown out or improved upon. There's a richness to all the smelly stuff that we so dislike and so little desire. The delightful things—what we love so dearly about ourselves, the places in which we feel some sense of pride or inspiration—these are also our wealth."[4] We can often learn the most about life and acceptance by getting in touch with and accepting ourselves exactly as we are, addicted and mentally different. It doesn't mean we're bad, or that we're less than other people. It's just another little piece of ourselves with which we get to work.

BACK TO GNOSTICISM

Consider, for example, that the early Christians were divided about who God was and what life as a Christian was supposed to look like. The Gnostics thought that this world didn't really matter and that the God of the Old Testament was evil.[5] The Orthodox contingent disagreed believing this world was good and that this world was the place to be. Unfortunately for

4. Chodron, *Start Where You Are*, 3.

5. For more on Gnosticism see Jonas, *The Gnostic Religion*.

the Gnostics, when the Roman Empire under Constantine adopted Christianity, the Gnostics were declared heretics and burned, along with most of their writings. We are fortunate today that we have the Twelve Steps, a way of life that doesn't condemn anyone, let alone burn them for their step work for Heresy.

But is God really evil? Is the world really evil? The world is incredibly beautiful if you stop to look at it. Sure, there is suffering, but there is also joy, life, and beauty. Part of mindfulness, or presence, is being aware of this beauty. Stopping and being in touch with the fundamental goodness of life is something that addiction and mental illness prevent. When we are caught up in delusions, psychosis, and depression, often we can miss the bird song, or the sun shining or the rain falling. When we are obsessing about how to overcome our overdrawn bank account, our partner who is lying to us, or our inability to adequately meet the needs of our family, sometimes the joy of having a bank account, having a partner, or having a family gets lost.

The purpose of life is to know the secret treasure of the Divine in the present moment, this hidden treasure of love and joy and beauty. Mindfulness is a way to do this, and it requires stopping, and pausing. Mindfulness, when practiced regularly, creates a cognitive, or mental space between the desire to use and the insanity of addiction, and the recognition of the hidden treasure of life in a way that opens doors for better choices. Part of the reason that there has been an increasing movement to link mindfulness to addiction recovery is that this space can be the removal of the desire to use, and the ability to better tolerate cravings without acting on them.

Love as a restoration to sanity is another way to think about the Second Step. Often there is a delusion that we are drawing from an internal well that is limited. Sufism teaches that this is false. A step further from the concept of no-self, the Sufi belief is that the actual reality of the human person is that we are one with the Divine. This unity with the Divine is our true nature and is the ultimate reality of the human person. When we are in the insanity of addiction, we often think that we are limited, we come from a limited self-concept. This creates self-obsession, holding onto the self, and clinging. In other words, this is the suffering we talked about in Step One. This self-obsession and delusion, this fear-based insanity, lies at the core of addiction. It is the mental and spiritual nature of the disease. However, there is a hidden treasure that lies beneath the illusions of the self that is limitless and all powerful. If you don't want to think of it as God, you can just consider it the underlying fabric of the universe. As Muslims believe, "Allah is an Odd Number."

There is ample evidence at this point that our minds are very powerful. If we are operating out of a limited self-concept, this is going to create problems. With Sufism, the Judeo-Christian-Islamic dependence on a Higher Power goes deeper to understand that this very power that we worship is at the core of the true self of everyone and everything in Creation. Selfishness and self destruction as a way of life come from the delusion that we are limited. This is juxtaposed with the attitude of giving and loving that comes from an attitude of unlimited resources.

Many feminists have discussed the reality of the "Other," the ultimate addictive insanity of interpersonal relationships. This is based on an alienation from the world that comes from a fundamental misunderstanding of reality. When we try to exert our self-centered influence out of fears of lacking something, we oppress people. As far as the Second Step, this has two sides. One is that we can get caught up, particularly as women, in a concept that we are able to solve this for other people. This leads to the insanity of codependency, which so often occurs with addiction. The Second Step involves believing that we cannot continue to solve other people's imbalances with our own sacrifices. Then, there is the insanity of other people thinking that they can satisfy their imbalances with other people. The two are interconnected. The reality of mindfulness is that it can bring light and space to just being ok, especially with the realization that we are actually a part of the greater universe. The truth can set us free.

Living in balance and harmony is a hallmark of the sanity that comes from recovery. Material addiction and the destruction of the planet go together. Greed and destructive insanity work hand in hand to destroy us and the planet. It is a part of a spiritual life to live simply. Simplicity and love are basic elements of the spiritual path.

MINDFULNESS AND THE SECOND STEP

There are many ways that we can be restored to sanity. One of these ways is through mindfulness, right mindfulness, a part of the eightfold path. One way to practice mindfulness is the mindfulness exercise earlier in this chapter. Another way that we can practice mindfulness and the Second Step is to use mindfulness to cut through the addictive chatter which can fill our minds if we are trying to break free of negative habits. We can do this by being mindful of the consequences of our actions, and not to be "insane" by repeating the same mistakes and expecting different results. We can use mindfulness by becoming aware when we are in a craving or having a desire to act out by coming back to her breath. We can identify, "Oh, there is a craving" and be present with it, be curious about it.

Once we are breathing and present, we can do what some people call "playing the tape all the way through." This entails looking at the consequences of our actions beyond just the fix that acting out gives us. For example, if we want to drink some vodka, we can ask ourselves, "What will happen after we drink it? Will we have a blackout? Will we be able to stop with just one drink? Will there be any negative consequences to drinking?" When we concentrate and become mindful of the total picture, we are often able to talk ourselves out of acting out on our addiction. This is itself a restorative to sanity.

Another way that we can become mindful, in connection to the Second Step, is to notice people, places, and things which are a Power greater than ourselves and can restore us to sanity. Sometimes this is as simple as a walk around the block. In terms of being restored to sanity by a Power greater than ourselves, the pure act of being mindful is a great place to start. We can simply tune into our breath, and the world around us through mindfulness. Often this restores us to sanity faster than anything else.

The Second Step doesn't have to be about God at all. It can just be the simple act of taking three conscious breaths. And the Power greater than ourselves can be anything from the Gnostic idea of a God apart from this world, to the Christian idea of Jesus, to total rejection of theistic ideas. It can be just a matter of faith that the present moment contains all we need, and the mindfulness to live in this moment.

SECOND STEP AND LOVING KINDNESS MEDITATION

Addiction and mental illness are based on a fundamental insanity about escaping from life. How do we get oriented towards being sane though? It can be very overwhelming. If the fundamental nature of the universe is love, as many people believe it to be, harmonizing with this underlying reality is a step in the right direction. Sitting quietly with the mantra, "May I be happy. May I be peaceful. May I be well." It is a simple act of self-love that can radically transform the rejection of reality inherent in insanity.

This harmonizing with love is a simple and profound movement towards personal, relational, and universal peace.

Feeling compassion for ourselves is much stronger than feeling hatred for ourselves. Self-hate is a debilitating experience that tends to freeze progress or turn back the clock on growth. Self-love can open the doors of possibility. It can be very difficult to love yourself or speak kindly to yourself. I worked almost exclusively on loving self-talk for several years in therapy. Choosing a loving phrase to say to yourself can be very important. Something simple like, "I like me" can totally transform your experience of life.

MINDFULNESS, GRATITUDE, AND THE SECOND STEP

The concept of believing in a Power greater than ourselves that can restore us to sanity goes back to the concepts of gratitude and patience again as well. Gratitude is a quick power that can restore us to sanity. Gratitude is a profound spiritual concept, yes, but it's also a great mental health intervention. Gratitude has been shown to improve sleep, reduce anxiety, reduce depression, improve happiness, improve personal relationships, and the list continues. A great and quick mindfulness exercise is to make a gratitude list. This can be something you write down on your phone, text to a friend, write yourself an email, or keep a journal. There are endless variations. Even just take 10 seconds and make a mental list of three things you are grateful for. I guarantee that it will work to improve sanity. It is another example, like mindfulness of the breath, of ancient spiritual wisdom that has been proven to be effective by modern science.

Niyyah: Step Three

Actions are but by intention and every man shall have
but that which he intended.
- SAYING OF PROPHET MUHAMMAD (PBUH)

Step Three prayer: Oh, Turner of hearts,
make my heart firm on the path.

THE FEELING OF POWERLESSNESS is a fact of life when one is diagnosed with mental illness and drug addiction. We are powerless over our diagnosis. No matter how hard we try, we cannot change the fact that we are addicts and that we are mentally different. If we find our spiritual roots and connect to them, though, we can begin to change the way we deal with these realities. The intention to make a personal commitment to this ongoing day to day process of change is embodied in the Third Step.

MOVING AWAY FROM SELF-WILL: DOCTORS AND SPONSORS

The Second Step gives us a direction for where we want to go and with a map to follow. The Third Step is the decision to start the journey. The Third Step states, "We made a decision to turn our will and our lives over to the care of God as we understood Him." We have chosen guides, perhaps in the form of a sponsor, a counselor, and/or a doctor. It is important to have a doctor and a sponsor because we need to make an attempt to decrease the amount of self-will in our lives. Our will took us to our bottom. We need people to help us learn to make decisions which will not be the same self-destructive decisions that we have made in the past. Listening to both our doctors and our sponsors gives us a great opportunity to get out of ourselves and our self-will.

The Third Step for me was very difficult because I kept making decisions to try really hard to be good and to be normal. As soon as I started trying to be normal, I would get frustrated and give up. I was working with doctors who were invested in getting me to "function normally." They often made disclaimers such as, "Oh what's normal," or "Define crazy," but the fundamental message they were sending was clear. They wanted me to learn to be more like other people. I resented this directive. At heart, I felt like I ought to be honored for the unique psychosis that I was exhibiting. When I was suicidal, it seemed like a very logical answer to the pain that I was in, yet they kept hiding the knives. The Third Step, happily, does not require me to do anything other than making the decision to trust the process of recovery enough to give life a chance.

In our addiction, we constantly have handed over control to our dealers, our drugs, the courts, the cops, the mental institutions, the psych wards. The Third Step asks us to hand over control to our spiritual roots. When we realize that despite the illusions we maintain, we are totally out of control really, we are in touch with Reality. It's natural to want to control things since most people do, but once we cross the line into addiction, we are out of control, even if it is only emotionally. Obviously, since there is no self, control is just an illusion. What really exists are fields of probability manifesting at our level—like cats and computers and Redwood trees. Within this field of reality, there is only interconnectedness. No matter how hard we try to control externals, we will fail, and we have already mentioned that there is no separation between us and anything else. Control is impossible, but one thing we do have the power to do is to be mindful.

We have the ability to make decisions. We can't control the outcome, but we have the power to make choices about our direction. If we have stopped using and started taking medication, working with the doctor, or otherwise confronting our mental challenges, we have already made an important decision.

In the process of recovery from mental illness, we often have to deal with a lot of doctors. Many doctors are hostile to treating mental illness with spiritual remedies. They are generally either closed to or covertly suspicious of anything that has to do with spirituality because the medical establishment sees much of mentally different people's connection to the Divine to be pathologically based. Fortunately, there are doctors who are more understanding, and there are many who are willing to learn. There is also an increasing amount of literature available on the topic

THE CENTRALITY AND IMPORTANCE OF INTENTION: NIYYAH

In Islam, intentions are of central importance. There is a saying of the Prophet (PBUH) that says, "Actions are but by intention and every man shall have but that which he intended." In other words, if you pursue the spiritual path because you want people to like you, that's the result you will get, or if you want to get rich, then that's what you will achieve. However, if you want to follow the spiritual path to achieve realization, peace, closeness to God, then that will be what you will achieve. The reward for an action in Islam is entirely based on the intention behind it.

There are many practices that form the basis of Islam, two of which are the five times prayer and fasting. For a prayer to be valid, there has to be a part which starts the prayer where the worshipper stops, and states the intention of which prayer they are praying, and that it is for God. Similarly, fasting in the month of Ramadan depends on intention. Every day that you fast, the night before, before midnight, you have to make the intention to fast the following day for Ramadan, for the sake of Allah. Without this intention, the fast does not count. All actions in Islam are valued entirely based on the clear statement of intention.

The Third Step involves decision-making. Many of us have been so institutionalized that we feel we have no power to make decisions. The Third Step is our opportunity to make a decision to commit to our spiritual roots. This commitment has been crucial to my recovery and I encourage all those who want to make it to do so.

To repeat, the Third Step states, "We made a decision to turn our will and our lives over to the care of God as we understood him." In our discussion of the Second Step, we talked about the fact that finding our spiritual roots is a personal process. In the Third Step, we turn our will and our lives over to these spiritual roots. The process of finding our spiritual roots is one of the most important parts of Twelve Step recovery, and it can be a huge aid in recovering from mental difficulties. One way to find these roots is to ask if there are any powers that bring us peace which are bigger than ourselves. It could be found through nature; it could be found through the Buddha or Jesus. I know one person whose God is his dog! What matters is that there is a voice of sanity in the midst of our lives which speaks to us about the world around us in ways that do not reflect our addiction.

We make a decision to turn our will and our lives over to the care of a greater power than ourselves. This doesn't have to be such a big deal. As the old joke goes, once there were three frogs sitting on the lily pad. Two decided to jump in. How many were left? The answer is that all three were left. The two just made a decision, but they didn't actually jump! The Third Step is a little intimidating because it seems like taking a monastic vow to be pure and holy for the rest of our lives, but it's just a new frame of reference that is bigger than our cramped world of addiction and dis-ease. It's a decision to open our minds and hearts to the world around us.

Making a decision to turn our will and our lives over to the care of God as we understood Him, Her, or It involves the commitment to the process of learning how to live in the world. Mental difference often alienates us from the world that the majority of people in Western society inhabit. We may reject them before they reject us, after a while, out of fear and pain. It is important to find people we can trust, especially a doctor, a sponsor, or counselor who can help us through the Twelve Steps.

TAKING REFUGE

How do we find the strength to stay out of self-will when we have existed in it for so long? In Buddhism, there is a process called taking refuge. The person takes refuge in the three jewels: the *Dharma*, the *Sangha*, and the *Buddha*. The *Buddha* is the teacher and the light of mindfulness in each of us. The *Dharma* is the path, and the *Sangha* is the community of people who are following the path.

In *Living Buddha, Living Christ*, Thich Nat Hahn (also known as Thay, or teacher) teaches "To take refuge in our mindfulness, our mindful breathing and the five elements that comprise our self."[1] When I do this meditation, I feel centered. I feel like I don't need to go running around to anyone or anything to try and fix the emptiness which I feel sometimes, and it can be very healing.

1. Hanh, *Living Buddha, Living Christ*, 121.

Christianity has a similar practice called the prayer of the heart where one repeats the name of Jesus in the heart and practices dwelling in the presence of God. In Christianity, there are also many wonderful prayers, and some of them can be heard in Twelve Step meetings. These practices are very grounding and can be a way to reaffirm one's connection to one's spiritual roots.

In Islam, there is also a daily process of taking refuge. One of the Five Pillars of Islam is praying five times a day. We bow to God and prostrate before God to remind ourselves that what the Quran calls the underlying reality, or Allah, is the most essential element of a happy life. It is very grounding to remember that we are not in control. All the chaotic mind states that life produces can become less invasive through the process of taking refuge. Imam Khorasani says, "Of course, when a person believes in God, and takes refuge in God from these experiences several times a day, placing himself near God's blessing, remembering God, surely He will help a person come to peace with himself."[2]

The point of taking refuge in these three traditions is to turn over control to a Power greater than our isolated egos. We learned in the first two steps that we are not in control, and a Power other than ourselves is the source of freedom. Taking refuge gives us the peace of knowing that there is a force acting for us that has our best interest at heart, that can take care of us when we cannot take care of ourselves. Whether this power is Allah, Jesus, or the Buddha isn't the main issue. The point is that we give up trying to control everything and everybody and let go of our egotistical agendas.

Chogyam Trungpa describes the development of ego in *Cutting Through Spiritual Materialism.*[3] One metaphor he uses is that when we are bound by our egos, it is often a big relief for us when we realize that in actuality, we are just a part of a larger whole. Almost every religion that I have ever encountered describes this larger whole as conscious. When we surrender to the desert and let go of our delusion of being the most important grain of sand, we feel a lot of relief. It is helpful to remember that if the gigantic endless desert of the universe has a mind, it can understand the whole picture better than just our little isolated self, buried in a heap of other grains of sand.

In times of extreme mental illness, it can be very difficult to have any hope. That is the most crucial time of all to practice the Third Step. When

2. Khorasani, *Way of Success and Happiness,* 69.

3. Trungpa, *Cutting through Spiritual Materialism,* 125.

the suicidal ideation becomes overwhelming, to simply make a decision to be mindful and to stay on the path with the rest of humanity can be a source of great strength. If we choose to believe in God, merely resting in the presence of the Divine with the intention to surrender to whatever comes with faith fills us with the power to do what otherwise might be impossible. Like the Second Step, the Third Step is a process. No one can perfectly adhere to the spiritual path. The decision to recommit must be made over the course of a lifetime, beginning again and again.

THE BHAGAVAD GITA: FACING THE BATTLE

Hinduism has a wonderful scripture called *The Bhagavad-Gita.* Ancient Hindu scripture was formed from a series of epics. There were stories of gods and heroes and wars and more. Well, in the middle of the big battle, the hero realizes that he is going to fight his family members. The story of his conflict over fighting them is the story of *The Bhagavad-Gita.* Krishna, an incarnation of the part of the Hindu Trinity who is the sustainer of the universe, Vishnu, is the man's charioteer. Arjuna, the warrior in conflict, is on the battlefield facing his cousins and uncles and other family members. In the face of overwhelming suffering that he knows is going to come from the battle, he despairs and lies down in his chariot. At this point, Krishna teaches Arjuna about the true nature of life. Krishna tells Arjuna how to live, how to attain freedom from the constant cycle of death and rebirth and how to overcome all suffering. *The Bhagavad-Gita* was the scripture that guided Gandhi's life. At the end of the discussion between Arjuna and Krishna, Arjuna stands up and faces the battle before him.

For many of us, when we reach the third step, we lie down in our chariots in despair. We can't fight the battle in front of us because we know that we are facing ourselves. Essentially, we are going to have to battle using the survival skills which have helped us deal with life up to this point. Well, these skills were useful in our disease, but they are a hindrance in our new way of life. We don't know how we can engage ourselves in the conflict of change, but it is required for recovery from the challenges of drug addiction and mental difference. The Third Step is like our conversation with our personal Krishna, God, as we understand God. The relationship we decide to develop with the spiritual life that we choose can become our strength and our inspiration to stand up and face the conflict that lies at our feet.

MINDFULNESS AND STEP THREE

Mindfulness relates to Step Three in a variety of ways. Try to notice as you go through your day when you are in your Higher Power's will, or in self-will. A great way to test this is to ask yourself, "If I was my own child, would I recommend the current behavior that I am exhibiting?" If not, you're probably not acting according to spiritual principles. Turning our will and our lives completely over to the care of our Higher Power is an ideal for which to strive. It takes time and practice to live in God's will. Try taking refuge in the moment and in your Higher Power's will for you. Try breathing mindfully if you're getting carried away by a craving or an urge to act out in a way that is destructive to yourself or to others. Remember that this is the hardest battle to fight since you're fighting yourself, and this has been true since ancient times as one of the hardest and highest callings of humanity.

In Islam, the tradition teaches us to be mindful about our intentions. This involves a continued process of clarifying our intentions so that we are aiming for the actual goals we want. Try to stop, as a process of Step Three, and figure out, "Where do I want to go? What do I want from life, and death? What do I want from today?"

MINDFULNESS OF GOALS: WRITE THEM DOWN!

There are studies that suggest that in life goal making is very important, and that people who write down their goals achieve them at a much higher rate than those who do not. Take time, perhaps, to write down a one-year, five-year, ten-year, twenty-year, and eternal plan. With that type of mindfulness, it is much easier to keep our intentions clear for ourselves. Part of the process of the steps usually involves a lot of writing so this process organically happens as a part of recovery to some extent. However, making it really crisp and clear can still add extra focus to our lives. There is an old saying in recovery that if a person was to enter recovery and make a list in the first few weeks of everything they could possibly want from recovery, and proceed to work the steps, if they only got every single thing on their list, they would have been selling themselves short. I encourage trying this practice.

PART TWO

Morality and the Fourth Step

Morality and the Fourth Step

Whosoever of you sees an evil action, let him change it with his hand; and if he is not able to do so, then with his tongue; and if he is not able to do so, then with his heart; and that is the weakest of faith.
- Saying of Prophet Muhammad (PBUH)

The Serenity Prayer: God, grant me the serenity to accept the things I cannot change, courage to change the things I can, and the wisdom to know the difference.

THE FOURTH STEP STATES, "We made a searching and fearless moral inventory of ourselves." The first three steps involved laying a foundation. The Fourth Step builds on this foundation. In the next four chapters, I will address two standards for morality: The Ten Commandments and the Five Wonderful Precepts of Buddhism and their relationship to the Fourth Step. This discussion will focus on a few factors involved in a moral inventory, but the process is not meant to be exhaustive. Usually, in the Fourth Step, we look at things like resentments, our relationships, including sexual relationships, our fears, our shame and guilt, our assets and our liabilities. The following sections of this book only touch on a few things which will make a Fourth Step easier when working with a sponsor. Living right is the focus of the next sections, again, not an exhaustive perspective on the Fourth Step inventory

JIHAD AN-NAFS

There is a widespread consensus among people in recovery that the Fourth Step is the hardest of the steps. This is traditionally because it requires the most soul searching and writing; it involves looking at realities that are challenging to face, how we have created the wreckage in our lives. here is a good story about the Prophet of Islam (PBUH). He and his companions were leaving a battle and he said, "You have arrived with an excellent arrival, you have come from the Lesser Jihad to the Greater Jihad—the striving of a servant of God against the desires." [1] While there is some dispute among some sources whether or not this is a valid report that the Prophet (PBUH) said this, Muslims often refer to self-purification as the Greater Jihad, and understand that the struggle to live a righteous life is the most important and central meaning for Muslims today.

To understand the idea of the spiritual struggle better, a discussion of the Islamic concept of the self is merited. First, the Greater Jihad is described as *jihad-an-nafs*. The *nafs* are a part of the self. The Self according to Muslim sources is composed of the heart, or *qalb*, the spirit, or *ruh*, the intelligence, reason, and mind, or *aql*, and the desires, drives and urges, or the *nafs*. These four parts of the self work together in harmony in a healthy person in relationship to God in a balanced and complete way.

The purification of the *nafs* is a progressive struggle. The *nafs* can be described as having stages in their development. There are three main stages: *nafs ammara*, *nafs lawwama*, and *nafs mutmainnah*. The *nafs amara* are the *nafs* of a person who is totally dissolute. They are a person with no self-control, who lives at the mercy of their urges and whims. The *nafs lawwama* is the accusing *nafs*, or the *nafs* in the process of improving where a person begins to struggle and strive to do better. The *nafs mutmainnah* is the peaceful *nafs*, the *nafs* that have been controlled, directed and peaceful, no longer chaotic but ordered.[2]

Dr. Nahid Angha, a modern-day mystic and scholar and founder of the International Association of Sufism, mentioned as one of the great women of Sufism in the book *Women of Sufism: A Hidden Treasure*,[3] wrote on the idea of purifying the *nafs* in her book *Principles of Sufism*. She states:

1. al-Qadir al-Jilani, *Secret of Secrets*, 33.

2. Angha, *Principles of Sufism*.

3. Helminski, *Women of Sufism*.

The desires of the *nafs* extinguish the light of divine love in the heart of the *salek*. A person who is searching for a spiritual path to ascend his being to a higher level has to cultivate higher qualities in his heart and mind and remain stable and strong at all times so not to become motivated by the lower qualities of the *nafs* such as jealousy, greed and envy. The lower and worthless qualities of *nafs* will disturb tranquility within, they become the chains fastening the human mind to the short lived waves of life and distract him from the essence of his being. To transform them into praiseworthy qualities will add to the peace and tranquility of the mind, thus leading the way to a truthful understanding of one's being. [4]

There is an analogy in Buddhism to the self as a chariot. Some people are lying down in the chariot, the horses are running wild, and the person is thrown around and destroyed. Then the person stands, and tries to control the horses and the chariot. The final stage is when the person has the chariot under control. This is a similar progression to the idea of the development of spiritual discipline through the purification and struggle with the *nafs*.

The Fourth Step is the beginning of the actual spiritual struggle in the Twelve Steps. It is the beginning of the ordering of the self in line with spiritual principles and away from the behaviors which characterize a self-centered, self-obsessed, destructive life. To really live a spiritual life requires this process of purification of the *nafs*, the progression of the self towards *nafs mutmainnah*.

The process of the Fourth Step is a process of purification of the *nafs*. This is a core concern of Sufism. Dr. Arife Ellen Hammerle describes the centrality of the purification of the *nafs* in her book *Sufi Grace: Sacred Wisdom Heart to Heart*. She says:

> The wisdom of Sufi teachings is devoted to reflecting the Divine light by polishing the mirror of the heart . . . .An unpolished mirror reflects merely images of who we *think* we are—reflections of personality and qualities to which we have been attached but are not real. This in Sufism is defined by the *nafs*—which when unpolished, creates a strong ego that blinds us to perceptions, thoughts, false ways of understanding who we are . . . We need to clean up the aspects of these patterns that are negative and false. Therefore, in Sufism we clean up the *nafs*.[5]

---

4. Angha, *Principles of Sufism*, 16-17.

5. Hammerle, Safa, Newman, and Pryor, *Sufi Grace*, 27.

The *jihad-an-nafs* is a core part of Sufism, and in some ways defines the work of the Twelve Steps. The Fourth Step, which many tend to dread or shy away from, is the foundation of this work. Therefore, when we avoid the Fourth Step, we avoid the actual process of change which has the power to transform us from people who we don't really want to be, to the people we dream ourselves to be.

SILA

In Buddhism, the eightfold path is divided into three major sections as we have discussed already. They are in the Pali, *panna*, or wisdom, *samadhi*, or focus and concentration, and *sila*, or right living and behavior. No one is suggesting that these pieces work independently of each other, of course; just that as people work through their progression on the spiritual path, these parts work together. The action of right living, or *sila*, is the focus of the fourth step. It is the work to bring life into alignment with spiritual principles, what is known in Islam as *jihad-an-nafs*. The purification of action is the basis of the purification of focus and wisdom.

THE INTERNAL FORM DEPENDS ON THE EXTERNAL FORM

One of the major themes for many addicts is that we are focused on spiritual realities. Particularly as mentally different, the spiritual plane is often more real for us than it is for other people. However, many of us have suffered intensely while using, in that we were unable to fulfill our goals to be spiritual due to our ongoing active addiction. Being clean is the first step towards a better spiritual life for many. Our ideas of spirituality, questions that we pondered intellectually, become lived realities. Instead of just valuing truth, we become honest people. Instead of valuing generosity while stealing, we begin to live lives of service.

One way that this has been expressed in Buddhism is the expression, "The elbow does not bend backward." The concept is that there is a boundary around what is possible in spiritual life. You wait for the light to change at the crosswalk and don't drive intoxicated. You speak kindly to others. You practice cash register honesty. These types of small changes form a structure for a genuine spiritual life.

In Sufism, there is a discussion that you cannot just believe in Islam, or just believe in God; you have to have the external form. You cannot profess faith but consider yourself above the law of God. Acknowledging the truth of God's universal light and love, according to many, requires living that as a practical form of daily existence. It can't just be a concept. It has to be practice.

Making this external life of obedience to the law of right and wrong a daily reality is the essence of Steps Four through Seven. Steps Four and Five involve discerning where there is need for change, and where we are succeeding. Step Six and Seven involve the committed refinement of our character according to these discoveries.

TURNING THE GAZE INWARD

Often people think that the primary struggle in life is against other people. The world is screwed up, and fighting against these outer problems is the goal of life. There is a tendency in our society to externalize personal focus, and it is a human tendency, made worse by Reality-TV culture, where living has been reduced to watching other people live on a screen while we sit in our living rooms. It is easy to blame other people, to resent people, and to attribute our problems to others with this type of voyeuristic attitude, and it is pervasive in our society, not confined to those who are regularly watching *Keeping up with the Kardashians,* but of a culture that has de-emphasized personal responsibility. Sometimes there is truth to the idea that other people have genuinely harmed us, and we are rightfully, justifiably upset. However, focusing on our part in situations is an empowering experience which restores control of our lives to us.

A central part of the spiritual life is to turn our gaze inward and begin to examine and methodically purify our lives. Just not using drugs and alcohol is a huge step in this direction. If we have established our sobriety after using drugs, we have taken a huge step in the right direction. Many of us lived our lives in addiction with intense heartfelt desires to be good and spiritual people. We sincerely desired to be spiritual people, and read spiritual books, or went to church or engaged in other spiritual practices. It is something to celebrate to just know that we have managed to get our feet firmly on the path of recovery and something that we can treasure and value, that no one can take away from us.

I have often compared it to a light that shines in my heart in the midst of trouble. Life can be falling apart, problems can be huge, but the knowledge that I have of my sobriety shines in my heart and gives me hope. Once we have this gift of sobriety, we can keep it as long as we choose not to pick up. No one can take it away from us.

When we begin to have the clarity that comes from recovery, we can use this light to illuminate a path to the spiritual life that so many of us have longed for so intensely. Spiritual life moves from a conceptual practice, where we theorize, and speculate, to a concrete practice of refining our lives so we become the people we have always wanted to be. The work of this movement from theorizing about being a good person, to actually being the people we want to be, gets underway in the Fourth Step inventory.

The path of Islam, and the path of Sufism specifically, involves a gradual progression towards a higher level of realization of the self. The first of these levels is the level of *sharia*, which is followed eventually after gradual evolution and work to the final station of *ma'rifah*, or divine wisdom.[6] The work to attain *ma'rifah* is the essence of Sufism, and in the end the realization of truth or *haqiqa*.[7] Recovery is a spiritual path, one that goes far beyond the simple relief from the compulsion to use drugs, or the insanity and unmanageability of out-of-control mind states. Abd al-Qadir al-Jilani states of the *sharia* and the rules and progress of the spiritual path through self-purification: "These are the general rules which apply to the material being of man. Then there is the spiritual being of man, or the spiritual man, who is called the pure man. His goal is total closeness to Allah. The only way to this end is the knowledge of truth (*haqiqa*). In the first-created realm of absolute being of oneness, this knowledge is called Unity."[8] He goes on to say of this process of self-purification, "True knowledge is the knowledge of Unity. The wise lover unites with his Beloved. From this material realm, flying with spiritual wings he soars to the realm of attainment, for the devout walk to Paradise while the wise fly to the realms close to their Lord."[9]

The work to purify the self is at its heart the first step in closeness to the Divine. This is the level of sharia. As the layers of harm to oneself and others get peeled away, like the layers of an onion, more are revealed. This process of uncovering is the process of self-discovery and development of

6. al-Qadir al-Jilani, *Secret of Secrets*, 14.

7. al-Qadir al-Jilani, *Secret of Secrets*, 14.

8. al-Qadir al-Jilani, *Secret of Secrets*, 14.

9. al-Qadir al-Jilani, *Secret of Secrets*, 16.

insight into our actions and motivations that is a tremendous relief and joy for most of us who have had high spiritual hopes but little ability to achieve them. As the layers peel away, the self is revealed as full of possibility, as the divine self which is at the core of us as human beings. This truth of self-knowledge, is the spiritual insight which can only be gained through the practical application of self-purification. The Fourth Step is a gift on the path that allows us to get the first levels of clarity about ourselves.

BLAME, SHAME, AND ACCOUNTABILITY

One of the ongoing debates in pop-culture about sin, corruption, and mistakes in life, revolves around blame and shame. For many people shame and self-blame run deep and go back to messages from childhood, or even exist at the genetic level. The Fourth Step is not meant to be about finding out how screwed up we are, and engaging in self-recrimination for our mistakes and failures. Blame and shame can be toxic forces that can substantially limit our ability to actually reach a place of accountability. They can be paralyzing and frustrating, debilitating mindsets that prevent and limit growth. In general, they are to be avoided in the process of the steps. This is not to say not to be emotionally accountable but to be present in a way that furthers growth, through self-love and self-compassion

BEING A SURVIVOR AND RESILIENCY

If the blame and shame problem was not enough, there is the problem that many people face that they were genuinely victims in the course of their lives. They experienced situations that they had no control over that led to further deterioration of their lives and actions. Being raped, molested, abused through physical, emotional, or verbal violence can cause such harm that they lead to a paralyzed sense of self, and an inability to make healthy sane choices.

If we have stopped using, and reached the place where we have begun a Fourth and Fifth Step, or even if you have just picked up this book and are thinking about embarking on the Twelve Steps as a process of change, one of the elements of self-love and self-compassion can involve taking the time to validate that just arriving here is a testament to our strength of character. We don't have to be perfect; in fact, we never will be perfect, but the fact that we have survived horrific situations to come to a point in our lives where we have prioritized our spiritual growth is a huge victory. Being here, now, even being willing to be present with the wreckage of our lives is evidence of our immense resiliency.

Chapter Four

Morality

> Worship God and associate nothing with Him, and to parents do good, and to relatives, orphans, the needy, the near neighbor, the neighbor farther away, the companion at your side, the traveler, and those whom your right hands possess.
>
> -QURAN 4:36

DESPITE THE FACT THAT the culture of the United States is predominantly Judeo-Christian, the majority of people cannot name the Ten Commandments. We all have some ideas of morals, though. Most cultures agree that lying, stealing, cheating, and killing are not ethical things to do. There are, of course, different variations on what constitutes unethical acts of these sorts between cultures. For example, for some people eating meat is killing, while for others it is not. For most of us, however, there is a general sense in our hearts of what is right and wrong. Many people who have very strong values are atheists. In fact, some of the most moral people I know are atheists. Morality does not have to do with a god, our religion, or anything doctrinal, necessarily.

As human beings, all addicts have a sense of right and wrong deep within their hearts, souls, and minds. Unfortunately, in the course of our addiction, we have often compromised those values in our search for the next high. The next few chapters concern themselves with reestablishing our sense of basic ethical values, now that we have put down the beginnings of our spiritual roots. The process of establishing our values happens gradually through the steps, but the Fourth and Fifth Steps are a crucial turning point. By examining what we feel good about in our lives, and where we feel we could have done better, we begin to see what our personal values are.

For me, the first Five Wonderful Precepts of Buddhism were the first set of religious rules which I felt I could aspire to keep. They dovetail in many ways with a message of the Twelve Steps. They include refraining from killing, refraining from stealing, refraining from committing adultery, refraining from wrong speech, and refraining from intoxicating substances. These precepts have become a defining force in my life. The nice thing about the Buddhist precepts is that there's no way to keep them perfectly. In the precept against killing, all beings are included. If you swat the mosquito, you have broken the precept. Although I am aware that mosquitoes are the primary pollinators of berries that I love, I just can't seem to have compassion for them when they are sucking my blood. I don't think that I ever will. However, I try to keep the precept in other ways such as eating vegetarian. Even as a vegetarian, I am killing the vegetables that I am eating, so unless I stop eating, I'm never ever going to be perfect about not killing, at least not in this life. All precepts are like that. There is no way to keep them without any flaw at all. We can try to keep them to the best of our ability, and that is the goal. Finding out what feels like the right balance is a very personal process.

LOVE AND PERSONAL TRANSFORMATION

The process of self-purification takes a great deal of work and dedication. We did not become addicts, or develop mental health challenges overnight, and we do not recover in a few days. The journey is lifelong. What can sustain us on this journey? Many of us have fallen into patterns of deep-seated self-hatred, and the process of taking a spiritual inventory can be experienced as a hostile work of self-recrimination and self-blame. But this is not the idea of self-purification in the Twelve Steps or in Sufism. The work of the Twelve Steps is a work of self-love, a profound gift that we give ourselves to live a better way of life, be better people, and love the gift of the present moment, our present experience, and the opportunities and challenges of each and every day.

It is a true statement that you can aggress yourself into health and change, or you can love yourself into a better person. In Sufism and the Twelve Steps, the process of self-purification is a process of love. It is an alchemical transformation of the self to a finer, more valuable substance. Amelia Pryor states, "On the path of Sufism love is the alchemy of transformation."[1]

THE TEN COMMANDMENTS

The commandments and the precepts have many commonalities since both teach that stealing, lying, killing, and harming others are wrong. The commandments, though, have a few added stipulations. The first two commandments that Moses gives to the Israelites in Exodus are, "You shall have no other gods before me," and "You shall not make yourself an idol in the form of anything in heaven above or on the earth beneath or in the waters below." The Third Commandment states, "You shall not misuse the name of the Lord your God." (Exodus 20: 1-2)

The first three commandments required that the Israelites keep their God in the center of their lives, totally holy, and totally transcendent. They are commandments against idolatry. Idolatry in those days involved worship of deities who bestowed favors upon the people such as money, sex, good crops, etc. The point of the commandment against idolatry was that the people were not supposed to pursue their own selfish desires from other gods. They were instructed to serve their God, not seek favors from other gods.

Often in the modern world, people seek money, power, prestige, and sex. The first three commandments instruct us to live a life of service rather than a life of feeding our egos. It is fair to say that most addicts have served the high that they got from drugs. They lied for it, stole for it, had sex for it, gave money for it, and some even killed for it. The first three commandments direct us against these behaviors

<hr>

1. Hammerle, Ali, Newman, and Pryor, *Sufi Grace*, 84.

THE CENTRAL COMMAND OF ISLAM: TAWHID

One of the most important things to understand about Islam is the centrality of the idea of *tawhid*. The commandment not to associate partners with God is the most important command and rule and precept of the religion. *Tawhid* has virtually endless implications for human life and society, but one is that we need to treat other people with respect. While Christianity taught that men were above women, and people were above nature, Islam teaches that we are all dependent on a radically transcendent Divine Oneness. This leads to an egalitarian sense of human society, where piety demands treating other people with respect. Part of taking an inventory of our wrongs involves dealing directly with how our disrespect of God has translated into concrete harms to our families and society.

The Fourth Step and the purification of the self is a route to understanding the fundamental Unity that is reality.

> Practices that aid in purifying the essence of one's self enable a person to understand the principle of Unity. When we understand the principle of Unity, and live according to that understanding, we experience inner peace and balance despite living in a world of changes and distractions. We gain compassion and respect for others, realizing that we are all connected to the whole of existence.[2]

Another important implication of Unity is that truly understanding Unity leads to freedom. Addiction, mental illness, and the corruption of the self that they produce leaves us in a state of confusion, brokenness, and bondage to the world. Without some work, we suffer the loss of our ability to work, learn, and be with our friends and families. It is a loss of our natural God given birthright as human beings. Understanding reality and getting rid of our idols and idolatry for a right understanding of the fundamental Reality of existence allows us to no longer be confused and swayed by the world. There is an Islamic saying that the world is like an ocean: you can sail on it, but don't drown in it. Part of not drowning in the world is understanding that the Reality of the Divine in all its transcendent majesty is the Truth of the Universe. This is Religion, and this leads to Freedom.[3]

---

2. Hammerle, Ali, Newman, and Pryor, *Sufi Grace*, 32.

3. Hammerle, Ali, Newman, and Pryor, *Sufi Grace*, 62.

A NOTE ON THE MEANING OF SIN

Another misunderstanding regarding Christian morality is that it is very judgmental, since many people do not understand the original meaning of the word sin. A lot of people think if you sin, you must be a bad person, that you must be intrinsically evil, and a lot of Christian religions say that we are sinners, and that must mean we're fundamentally screwed up and bad. An understanding of sin as a mistake rather than a permanent moral scar can help in this matter. If we believe that everything is divinely ordained, it is an act of extreme ego to think that God's plan has somehow gone wrong. We can just hope that we do more esteemable acts in the future so that we can eventually have self-esteem.

SERVICE

Service to others is a great way to start doing esteemable acts. An important way to stay away from drugs is to live the kind of selfless life that is so foreign to us when we are in our addiction. If we agree that idolatry is serving our own little egotistical agendas, then service is a great way to stop being idolatrous! Service can range from doing the dishes that your roommate left in the sink, to picking up litter when you're on a hike, to taking a job at a Twelve Step meeting like making coffee or putting out literature.

FUNDAMENTAL GOODNESS OF HUMANITY
AND THE DIVINE WITHIN

It is clear in the Bible that people, while totally flawed, were created as a good work of God. In the beginning, according to the Bible, God created people and "saw that it was good." Of course, we know now that we evolved from the primordial ooze, so many people think that Genesis is a little outdated, kind of like the flat Earth Society (it really exists and has members). But many cultures have creation stories, and they are mostly saying that people are fundamentally good.

Buddhism definitely teaches this. It is the belief in Buddhism that we all contain the Buddha nature. If you really want to attain enlightenment, you can. Well, Jesus taught that too. He taught that we all had the Kingdom of God within us. It is well documented that Buddhist missionaries reached Palestine in Jesus' day. This statement seems to reflect a Buddhist understanding of the self as being fundamentally good, and the most important place to start looking for God. Jesus thought that all people were children of God, as he was. We all have access to the Divine; all we have to do is take the time to connect with it.

It is common during psychosis to experience intense feelings that we are special, divine, chosen. Some people think that they are Jesus. I met a guy who told me he was John the Baptist. I think these experiences reflect an intuitive sense that we are truly children of the Divine Consciousness and Mind behind the amazingly beautiful universe that we observe. The idea that the Kingdom is within us is simply manifesting in a way people are not familiar with because our consumer culture teaches us to look outside ourselves for the Divine.

HONORING OUR MOTHERS AND FATHERS

The commitment to honor one's father and mother can be useful, but it can be difficult. Many people today have had very abusive childhoods. While this is not my story, I have heard about it from people who endured foster care, or other challenges. How can they honor people who neglected them or hurt them in other ways? One of the gifts of life is the idea of our chosen family versus our biological family. We can often choose to honor our spiritual ancestors, our teachers, or our sponsors. The point is to become connected to the past in a way that is meaningful, but we are not living in a bubble on the planet. We have to coexist with the rest of the beings around us, and we can honor all of them as our fathers and mothers at one time or another.

HONORING THE SABBATH

The commandment to honor the Sabbath day concerns taking time out for God. Now, if we believe God is within, and that God is imminent in the universe, we can do this in a variety of ways. We can take the time to go for a walk and get in touch with our spiritual roots. We can take the time to stop running around being crazy, and we can just rest in the presence of our Higher Power

CONCLUSIONS: PRECEPTS VS. COMMANDMENTS

I wanted to discuss the commandments because I think so much of Judeo-Christian doctrine is misunderstood, and so many people, at the same time, come from the spiritual tradition. At least you have my perspective on it. The main reason that I have chosen to speak on the precepts rather than commandments is that I believe some people feel a sense of fear when confronted with the God of the Bible. The precepts, on the other hand, urge us to act out of love for our Buddha selves and the Buddha selves of others. I personally feel that the commandments can be a little intimidating. Because I am more comfortable with the precepts, and work with them more, I will discuss them as a possible starting place for ethical conduct. They are all about living right, and that is ultimately the goal of recovery

MINDFULNESS AND THE COMMANDMENTS

To follow any set of religious laws, we have to be mindful of our behavior and the way we live in the world. To be spiritual is an action that requires time, effort, and attention. One addict that I know asks herself the question, "Can I afford this right now?" before she acts. Most of us as addicts don't think before we act. We are impulse driven. This is true of people who have mental differences too. In mental difference, often the part of the brain that deals with decision-making is affected. We can't seem to control our impulses. Asking if we can spiritually afford to take an action before we make a move can be a helpful way to moderate the impulse driven nature of our minds.

In the course of learning right living, we have to learn to be mindful of our behavior. Before we act out by disrespecting someone, we can ask, "Can I afford this right now?" If the action is spiritual, then we probably can. If the action is unspiritual, an act of disrespect for ourselves, other people, or our Higher Power, then the answer is probably no. I would suggest that we all would be better off if we ask ourselves this question more often before acting out.

The deeper level from action to words is thought. If we are wallowing in resentment or self-pity, we can look at our emotional state and ask ourselves if we can afford to indulge the mind state that we are in. Action which is destructive often comes from thoughts which we have harbored which are unspiritual. Resentment, self-pity, and all sorts of other defects of character need to be healed at the source, in our minds and hearts. One tool which I use when these feelings are overwhelming is to take five minutes and really indulge the feeling and then move on.

Being mindful of our thoughts and actions is the beginning of true spiritual practice. It takes concerted effort and dedication to go from a life of resentment, self-pity, and disease to a life of freedom, health, and spiritual fitness, but being mindful of ourselves and asking ourselves about the consequences of our actions is the first step.

NOT TAKING ANYTHING

> Righteousness is good morality, and wrongdoing is that which wavers in your soul and which you dislike people finding out about.
> -Saying of Prophet Muhammad (PBUH)

When I was first diagnosed with mental illness and drug addiction, I did not want to be clean. I only wanted to get well enough to convince my family that I could return to the East Coast for school. As a result, the decision not to take drugs was made under duress, not for my own well-being but for ulterior motives. I also felt that my mental condition was not a problem. I regularly saw angels, and had drastic divine revelations. When I was hospitalized, I was given medication. I spit it out at first, but once I began to take my medication, I could no longer remember my dreams which had previously been vivid, prophetic, and very informative. I was attending Twelve Step meetings and had heard of the concept of total abstinence. I equated medicine with drugs and refused to take the medication.

Following my third departure from the hospital, and against medical advice, I tried to attend school and meetings without the aid of medication. I became so wrapped up in my own reality that I could no longer even have conversations with people. When I dropped out of college the second time, I committed myself to a psychiatric institution, but still refused medication on the grounds that it meant taking drugs. After some time in the institution, there was no change in my condition, and they told me that I would have to begin taking medication, or I would have to leave. I had a choice: either go to the streets, or acquiesce. I chose medication.

There is a great deal of ignorance both within and without the Twelve Step community about psychiatric medication. Psychiatrists themselves understand some of how it works, but the brain is so little understood that much of it remains guess work. The most important thing to understand about the difference between medication and drugs is that medication, when taken according to prescription, does not get you high. In fact, not taking medication can lead to greater altered states of consciousness than taking it. I say this from personal experience and conversations with other recovering people on psychoactive medication.

NOT TAKING ANYTHING WHEN YOU TAKE MEDICATION

Not taking anything, the zero step of recovery, can be much more complicated than it first appears when we are in a position where we need regular medication. It is important to take medication according to prescription, and under the supervision of the doctor. I personally have had a range of bad experiences with medication, including overdosing. Not taking my meds, and self-medicating with other drugs—all of these behaviors can be addictive. It continues to be a challenge for me to this day. Staying on top of medication, taking it properly, on schedule, always getting refills on time, etc., can be a challenge. Again, the Buddhist principle of mindfulness is so applicable. In monasteries, there are rules for eating, washing bowls, sitting meditation, and working in the garden. In many institutions, the call for meds is the same way. It's just a part of the daily act of recovery, and the time to get in touch with the moment.

Often, people feel shame that they need to take medication to counter their minds and emotions. Mental illness is not like diabetes—mental illness is stigmatized to an extent that no other illness can match. Working through shame can be a big factor in learning how to deal with medication. Getting in touch with the feelings of low self-esteem can be healing. Hopefully, if you are on medication, and you have a psychiatrist to talk to, then this is a good topic to work on

TOTAL ABSTINENCE

In addition to taking our meditation, we need to learn how not to take drugs one day at a time. Total abstinence from intoxicating substances is one of the Five Wonderful Precepts of Buddhism. It is the spiritual principle of Buddhism that intoxicating substances impair our ability to be present and cause great harm to society. Obviously, for the mentally ill, proper medication can also increase our ability to be present. The Fifth Precept, refraining from intoxicating substances, is a great spiritual practice in and of itself.

Many people feel that there are some substances which are intoxicating but can be very spiritual. For many Rastafarians, for example, cannabis is considered a sacrament. My opinion on this is a simple analogy: Just because Jesus told the disciples to drink wine in memory of his death at the Last Supper is no excuse to become a wino. Marijuana, indubitably, has a great number of healing properties. When I was in Nepal, the people carrying burdens on the trails, porters, smoked herb every day for their arthritis, the results of walking bent over with baskets and piles of wood on the back hanging from straps on their foreheads. All well and good. I doubt that my grandmother will take up the practice, but it would help her glaucoma. Unfortunately, for most addicts, marijuana is difficult to use medicinally because of the psychologically addicting properties. As some people say, "I only smoked pot once, every day for 20 years." It can also be a gateway drug. The experience of most recovering addicts is that total abstinence is the key to total freedom.

The spiritual purpose of marijuana, as I understand it in Rastafarianism, is that it is the tree of life; it could transform our planet. It could provide fuel, paper, and many other things which we are destroying in the environment trying to get high in other ways. It has great potential for helping society as a renewable resource, and for this reason, it can be seen as the light hope.

I personally am in favor of ending the drug war, and in support of treatment and rehabilitation. The criminalization of the disease of addiction has rapidly filled our prisons to overflowing. As recovering addicts, we can work towards the goals of treatment without harm by becoming many revolutionaries and carrying a message of recovery rather than incarceration.

It is a principle of Islam that alcohol and intoxicants are prohibited and cursed.[4] The prohibition against intoxicants, or *khamr*, in Islam, like the prohibition in Buddhism, encourages many people to be abstinent. It is part of the beauty of recovery to be able to follow this prohibition which so many of us are familiar with, and have struggled with. The benefits of a

4. Badri, *Islam and Alcoholism*, 3-7.

totally abstinent life are too numerous to count, but one of the main ones for a lot of people is the peace of mind and self-esteem that comes from the esteemable act of knowing that one is following this religious rule, the same in both Buddhism and Islam.

There are actually Twelve Step organizations that specifically focus on Islam like Millati Islami which you can find online and has groups that meet via Zoom. I need to make clear that I have no personal connection to Millati Islami, and this is not a paid or connected endorsement, but out of respect for the Muslims who are working on the Twelve Steps it is important to alert my readers to their existence. The congruence of Islam and the Twelve Steps aided me in becoming a Muslim, as I was in recovery for several years before I converted to Islam. However, for me personally, my path with the Twelve Steps has increased my ability to practice Islam as it has allowed me to live my religion with fewer sins. Being abstinent is a good part of any spiritual path, as mental clarity and focus aid and increase spiritual understanding. The legal prohibition of intoxicants in Buddhism and Islam supports this.

RECOVERY AS LIBERATION THEOLOGY

In South and Central America, there is a mass movement called Liberation Theology.[5] Most theologies and spiritual talk among Christians have historically been a top-down process. People in power tell the dispossessed what to believe, how to behave, and how to understand God, and the oppressed try to follow instructions. Liberation theology, on the other hand, is a bottom-up process. First, people go out into the community and work with the poor, the suffering, the sick, the people who aren't getting heard. They take scripture with them. In groups called Base Communities, the peasants of South and Central America have been working to transform their society through the spiritual principles of liberation contained in the Bible. Then, theologians talk about the process of liberation, and advocate for the poor amongst the people in power.

Twelve Step recovery is very similar to Liberation Theology in that it is a network of people trying to improve their lives through spiritual understanding and spiritual action. We can become liberation theologians by working to free our consciousness from a culture that criminalizes

5. For more on liberation theology see Berryman, *Liberation Theology*, and Gutierrez, *We Drink from Our Own Wells*.

difference, disease, and poverty. In the process, we have the potential to transform society. The simple act of not taking anything is a radical spiritual act. Our entire culture is a culture of consumption. Corporations routinely steal, lie, and manipulate to get what they want, with no concern for the welfare of others. We as individuals have the power to break radically with consumer culture by deconstructing the ideology that glorifies sedation through alcohol, drugs, and unhealthy consumption of all types.

NOT TAKING LIFE AND NOT STEALING

Two more Buddhist precepts are concerned with not taking anything, the First and the Second. The First Precept teaches to refrain from taking life, and the Second Precept teaches to refrain from stealing. In the process of drug addiction, any of us can become outlaws. We took what we wanted, and we didn't care who got hurt. Recovery involves a change in living style. The Fourth Step involves an inventory of where our lives have not lived up to our ethics. In the process, we come closer to knowing ourselves and being able to live up to our highest goals. Before we were obsessed with ourselves, but now, we try to think of others. We address the harm that we have done to our families. We can also address the harm that we have done to the world at large through killing and stealing

NOT TAKING CAFFEINE OR NICOTINE

Not taking anything is further complicated by the problem that two drugs are sanctioned by many Twelve-Step fellowships: coffee and nicotine. It is a hard decision to make whether to tackle these issues when we have been making such great changes. Is it worth it? For those of us with mental illness, cigarettes and coffee can be even more dependency inducing. Nicotine is a thought organizer, and 95% of schizophrenics are not only smokers, but also heavy smokers. Nicotine, by the way, is the only drug which is both an upper and a downer, so people who are bipolar can manage their mood swings through cigarettes. Depression has also been linked to smoking. Most people in the field of addiction recommend quitting smoking as part of a healthy program of recovery because studies have shown that people who quit smoking have a higher chance of staying clean than those who don't. If you can quit smoking, it is beneficial and healthy, but many people in recovery remain smokers for a while and quit gradually. This was my story. I smoked heavily in the first part of my recovery and quit smoking when I had been clean for several years. There is not just one right way to address nicotine addiction, so it is important to find the solution that works for you. In quitting smoking, there are many things which can aid in the process like nicotine replacement therapy and medication. It is helpful to talk to a doctor and get support for quitting smoking from a professional.

NOT COVETING AND GREED

The final commandments, the last two, both relate to coveting. Not coveting is a basic law of spiritual practice that appears throughout the Quran as well, in the injunction not to strain our eyes towards other people's worldly wealth. (Quran15:88, Quran 20:131) The idea that we should be satisfied with what God has blessed us with in this life is a basic concept of godliness. Jealousy, greed, envy, coveting, and all the negative and destructive consequences of these personality traits can cause so much damage.

There is an old saying that we should find satisfaction and encouragement by judging our material success by those who have less than us, and spiritual accomplishments by those who are ahead of us. If we become self-satisfied with our religious practice, consider all the great people who have far outpaced us for a dose of humility, and when we become despairing about our problems, look at people who suffer from war, or hunger, or the many major problems that some people are struggling with, and be grateful.

One of the beautiful prayers of Islam is, "Oh Allah, I am pleased with Allah as my Lord, Islam as my religion, and Muhammad as my prophet (PBUH)." When we can pray this, we can remember the gifts we have. Just being clean and not having to use one day at a time is something that any person in recovery can appreciate. It is such a gift just to have freedom.

GENEROSITY

Generosity is a spiritual principle that helps to fight the *jihad-an-nafs*. The movement of the heart to be happy for others is a beautiful gift we can give ourselves. When we find ourselves being jealous, we can practice a Buddhist principle which cures jealousy and can make life so much better. We can smile and appreciate that the other person has this gift and be happy for them. When we find happiness in other people's success, the world is such a better place. Smiling from the heart and the internal organs with joy for someone's large family, beautiful new car, Ph.D., or fantastic job or new accomplishment can give us an opportunity to expand our hearts so that we are more loving and giving all the time. It is worth the joy of being able to share in people's happiness, as it makes us have so many more opportunities for happiness. This principle in Buddhism is called sympathetic joy, or *mudita*, and it is one of the Four Noble Abodes, or Brahmaviharas. It is one of my favorite Buddhist principles.

CROSSING THE RIVER VS. CONVERSION

One of the things about Buddhism that I love is the metaphor of the raft. The three major schools of Buddhism have been called the little raft, the big raft, and the diamond raft. People who begin to practice Buddhism are called "Stream Enterers." Buddha says the teachings would be like a raft that you used to take you across the river of suffering. He obtained enlightenment on the other side and supposedly, once you get there, you don't need the raft anymore. But the reason I mention this is that many people feel like spiritual paths involve conversion. We just roll over one morning and 'blammo,' we are saved. Buddhism isn't like this at all. We see the river. We decide that we want to cross it, we enter the stream, and we work our way across. Maybe we reach the other side in this life, maybe we don't, but it was always the promise of another attempt in the next incarnation.

Christianity is the predominant religion of the United States, and it is the religion which provides most of the dominant culture's language about spirituality, but it is much more drastic. You are either in or you're out. Saved or Damned. There's not really much getting your feet wet, at least there wasn't traditionally, unless you were getting ready for full immersion into baptism which I have done. Islam is the same way. Additionally, Christianity looks to the afterlife as a time of judgment, and this produces a lot of pressure. If you don't get it right this time around, oh well. Burn. If you were Catholic, you might get to hang out in purgatory. This kind of attitude, still present among many Christians today, is very threatening. Personally, I don't see God as working that way, but a lot of us were raised with that picture. That's why Buddhism can be such a relief. We can hang out by the river bank and hop on the raft whenever we feel like starting. By analogy, not taking anything is a good way to get out onto the river, but we don't have to be perfect. The river is really, really big.

MINDFULNESS AND NOT TAKING ANYTHING

As you have begun to breathe, you have probably begun to notice your cravings. The next time you have a craving, feel it and breathe. If it is a craving for nicotine, wait a minute to smoke. Be mindful of your craving. Feel it. Then make a choice if you are going to act on it. A craving for drugs is the same way. If you feel a craving for drugs, notice it, and make the decision not to act on it. Play the tape all the way through. Think about the consequences of using. Learn what your triggers are. Notice what time of day you have cravings, what emotional state that you were in when you have them. Then you can begin to work with your triggers.

If you have lost the craving for drugs and for all other substances, notice your mental difference and how it affects your life. Notice when you are in an altered state. Notice your symptoms. Don't judge; just sit with them and experience them. As you learn to be present with yourself as you are, then comes the power to make choices. One way to prepare for the Fourth Step is to begin to see when we're taking drugs and how it has affected others. In being mindful of our impact on the world, we can begin to decrease the number of times we live in ways that go against our spiritual values.

Chapter Five

Listening and Speaking
The Ethics of Speech

Let him who believes in Allah and the Last Day either speak good
or keep silent.
-SAYING OF PROPHET MUHAMMAD (PBUH)

Three-fold Speech Test: Is it true? Is it kind? Is it necessary?

WHAT IS RIGHT SPEECH?

The Fourth Precept in Buddhism is to refrain from telling lies or the principle of right speech. This precept can be practiced as both speaking and
listening. In a similar way, Twelve Step recovery involves a lot of listening,
and, for some people, a lot of talking. When mental illness is added to the
equation, and as a result of therapy, speaking and listening become activities with which we can pass many hours of our week.

Refraining from wrong speech has three facets: first, not telling lies,
second, not exaggerating, and third refraining from filthy speech. This
may seem straightforward at first, except that for many of us we're so
accustomed to lying during our addiction that we didn't even know the
truth. This is why the Fourth Step is so essential. Through the process of

84

the Fourth Step, we learned to tell the truth to ourselves. In the Fifth Step, we tell the truth to someone else. By doing the Fourth Step, we become clearer about what is real, what exaggeration is, and what truth really is. The Fourth Step we work is often only a little glance at the truth, actually. The process of becoming honest takes work, and time. It can begin by learning how to listen to ourselves and to be honest about how we're feeling without trying to change it with drugs. That can be very spiritual. Just learning to identify a feeling can be a challenge if we have been high for so long that we have lost the ability to feel normally. Our society is constantly telling us to change the way we feel. Every ad seems to tell us that if we just get the right clothes or car or whatever, we'll be okay. We don't even know what okay it is, but we are chasing after some image that the media provide for us. If we have rejected mass media, then we aspire to feel the values that our particular subculture glorified. Many of us lose the ability to just accept our feelings as they are.

Dwelling in mental difference can also be a way to escape from what we are feeling. For me when I am hallucinating, I am feeling, but I am not feeling anything connected to the world that I share with other human beings. Learning how to sit still and breathe and identify said, scared, nervous, happy, joyful, excited, anxious, tired, that can be a challenge. But we have to stop lying to ourselves and get honest with who we are and what we are as part of our emotions.

Buddha taught that there were five *skandhas* or heaps, which make up the human person. The five heaps were feeling, perception, disposition, consciousness, and the form of the body.[1] Feeling is an important part of the self for Buddhists; however, as addicts we have totally cut ourselves off from this part of ourselves. In recovery, we have the opportunity to reconnect to this element of the self, and we have to be honest and mindful to do so

AS-SAMI: SPEAKING AND LISTENING AS MINDFULNESS OF GOD

The basic importance of speaking and listening is a practice that also relates to the Divine. Dr. Amelia Pryor talks about the importance of speaking and

---

1. Kalupahana, *History of Buddhist Philosophy*, 69. You can also find an extensive discussion of the ramifications of the doctrine of the *skandhas* throughout Trungpa, *Cutting through Spiritual Materialism*.

listening in several ways. One is that God is *As-Sami*, or the All-Hearing and our actions with our speech impact our relationship to God.[2] There are multiple hadith that focus on speech. One I focus on is, "Speak good or keep silent." Another that I think about is the hadith where the Messenger of God (PBUH) was talking about how to live a good life and go to heaven, and he grasped his tongue and said, "Restrain this." The companions asked him if the tongue was important and he said, "Is there anything that topples people on their faces - or he said on their noses into Hell-fire other than the jests of their tongues?"

The idea that our speech is a central part of the spiritual path was something my teacher taught me, in fact, it is one of the lessons he taught me that I think about most often. He told me a story about when he went to a craft store and saw a lot of artificial flowers that he liked. The sales lady was so happy at the way he complimented her on the flowers that she gave him arm loads of them. He used them to decorate his mosque, also known as the Redwood Mosque, or the Center for Peace and Compassion. He talked to me about how your tongue creates your reality. He also talked about how there are different ways to be in the world and who you are is determined by your speech. He stated that some people, based on the ugliness of their words, are like toads, or bugs, and some people are like flowers or butterflies. He said, "Be a butterfly."

IDENTITY

The Dalai Lama states that all people share the fundamental commonality that we want to be happy and avoid suffering; in other words, we want to feel good. But each of us has gender, class, racial, and sexual preferences which cause us to feel unique, and give us a unique orientation on the world. The movements for equal rights for people of color, women, lesbian, gay, bisexual, and transgender people have only just begun. It wasn't until the 1920s that women in the US got the right to vote, and only a mere 50 years ago that the civil rights movement took place. There is still a lot of discrimination to be faced.

Some people want to brush all this clambering for equal rights under the carpet and pretend that it does not exist. Some people think that if we don't talk about the problems, they will just go away. Unfortunately, that's like ignoring a roof that you know is leaking until the storm hits, and then

2. Hammerle, Ali, Newman, and Pryor, *Sufi Grace*, 112-116.

realizing you have to fix it when it's pouring rain on you. Why not fix the roof in the summertime on your day off?

Unfortunately, the problems of racism, homophobia, sexism, and classism are much worse. They are like an unsound foundation built in a house in California. When the earthquake hits, if anyone is inside, there's going to be trouble.

One thing we can all do to remedy the problems of racism, homophobia, classism, sexism, or oppression of any type is to figure out first who we ourselves truly are. We can be honest about our identity. We can see what qualities define us. We can own our right to be who we are.

The next step, the part that comes from listening, is the really transformational part. We can listen to who everyone else is. Haile Selassie, the former ruler of Ethiopia, said that there would be war until the color of a man's skin was of no more significance than the color of his eyes. When we listen to who people are, we may be able to stop judging them based on superficialities such as skin color, or clothes, or what kind of car that they drive. We can honor all beings without discrimination for whom they are, as unique and different. African American writer Audre Lorde (2007) says,

> Institutionalized rejection of difference is an absolute necessity in a profit economy which needs outside surplus people. As members of such an economy, we have all been programmed to respond to the human differences between us with fear and to handle that difference in one of three ways: Ignore it, and if that is not possible, copy it if we think it is dominant, or destroy it if we think it is subordinate. But we have no patterns for relating across our human difference as equals.[3]

As Lorde has observed, "Somewhere, on the edge of consciousness, there is what I call a *mythical norm* which each one of us within our hearts knows that is not me."[4] In America, this norm is usually defined as white, thin, male, heterosexual, Christian, abled, and financially secure. Many of us discovered as children that we already did not fit that mold. I personally was too strong a feminist to ever fit into the fifth-grade mode of thinking. That is my first remembrance of feeling different. Even white, straight, Christian, and financially secure thin men sometimes feel like they're too short! Everyone can feel different for one reason or another. We need to

---

3. Lorde, *Sister Outsider*, 115.

4. Lorde, *Sister Outsider*, 116.

stop and listen to ourselves and to each other as people and honor what we find.

This is not a call for everyone to go around asking each other, "How do you identify? Will you please educate me about your marginalized experience?" I say this especially to white people. Identity is something that we are forced to live with, and it is often a painful, volatile subject which makes religion and politics look like a discussion of tomorrow's weather. However veiled and tactful the couching, it is not a good idea. The point of this discussion is more to address the fact that with in the incredible diversity of the postmodern experience, identity has become a topic which I believe is not to be ignored, and when we think about speaking and listening deeply, we each come from a place in the rainbow which is totally unique and needs to be honored as such. We are totally at the mercy of our subjectivity, and until we recognize that, we can't listen.

A lot of people try to listen but often end up either giving advice or pointing fingers. When we're grounded in who we are as individuals, and aware of the multiplicity of experiences, we begin to see that we may have what seems to be the right answer for us, but it may be totally wrong for someone else. There's an old psychotherapy tactic of communicating with "I feel" statements rather than "you make me feel" statements. For example, when my roommate doesn't do her dishes, it's more productive for me to say, "I feel anxious when there are dishes in the sink, and I feel no desire to do them because they're your dishes. Would you please do your dishes?" rather than to say, "You make me so angry when you don't do the dishes." The first statement explains, while the second one is accusatory.

I believe that when we are secure in our identity then we can respect diversity. This kind of approach is easier because we can see people more the way the Dalai Lama does: all beings who want to be happy and avoid suffering.

DOCTORS, SPONSORS, AND MEETINGS

Right speech does not end with being honest with ourselves, and about who we are. We also have to be honest with our sponsors and our doctors. At times, I have detested my doctors. I actually used to fall asleep in therapy, yet it is important that we learn to talk about what is going on within us with someone else. When in the grasp of mental illness, it can be very hard to get in touch with reality. Our perceptions, another *skandha*, can become very distorted. We may think something is purple when in fact it is fluorescent green. Reality checking with our doctors can be a huge step toward developing a more accurate picture of the world.

At some point, we have to hone our listening skills. It is as important to listen when practicing right speech as it is to be able to speak. You may not trust your doctors. You may be afraid they're conspiring against you, if you're anything like me. Doctors often dismiss our perceptions in ways that feel hurtful. Once, I was having a very powerful and emotional re-union with one of the voices that I have been hearing in my head. He had returned after being gone for quite some time, and I was ecstatic. I cried and laughed, and I was so happy about it. I went into my doctor's office and enthusiastically related my experience. She suggested that I follow up on some psychiatric testing that I had been talking about.

Now, maybe your doctors are more sensitive, and in all honesty, that doctor helped me quite a bit to learn to accept myself, and learn to love being in the skin that I'm in. But maybe your doctor doesn't listen, or dismisses your experience. If you are working with a doctor who does not listen to you, it invalidates your experiences, so I strongly recommend that you find a new doctor. There is an abundance of psychologists, psychiatrists, MFFCs, Ph.D.'s, all sorts of people out there willing to take your money and listen to you. There are resources, in fact, for therapists and psychiatrists who have training in Buddhist or Islamic principles and a spiritual practice if that is appealing to you. Don't settle.

If you have found someone whom you can trust, then you can practice deep listening. Often, our doctors can offer insight into clinical conditions which we might not be as familiar with. They can also give us a sounding board for our ideas and teach us to better identify how we are actually feeling, and how accurately we are perceiving the world. With the help of a doctor, often we can make progress beyond our wildest dreams, and realize our wildest dreams.

Meetings also give us the opportunity to listen and speak deeply. Opening our ears and minds to the thoughts being shared around us can be deeply transformative, especially when we realize that so many people have felt what we've felt, done what we've done, been where we've been, and learned to live in the world in a way that is no longer self-destructive.

When I am feeling super spiritual, I meditate in meetings. The feeling of connectedness that comes from this practice fills the spiritual void within in a way that few other practices do.

TRUTHFULNESS AND RIGHT SPEECH

Part of speech is that it wells up from our hearts. The Bible relates that Jesus said, "It is not what goes into a man that defiles him but what comes out of a man." (Mark 7: 14-20) He meant that what people speak and do proceeds from their hearts and defiles them from the fact that they are unclean internally, in response to the multitude of rules on cleanliness observed by the Jewish people in his time. Similarly, "The honest person is one who possesses both outwardly apparent and inwardly sanctified sincerity and truthfulness. His honesty does consist in merely telling the truth, but in the inner character that makes truth possible."[5]

MINDFULNESS AND RIGHT SPEECH

The next time you're at a meeting, or in the group, try to listen carefully as you can to everything that is said, from the readings to each person who speaks. Make a decision not to speak. Listen deeply. Then begin to hear your own distraction and quiet through your breath. As you wander away from what is being said, simply tell yourself, "Thinking," or "Judging," and come back to listening.

5. Angha, *Principles of Sufism*, 54.

Chapter Six

A Few Words on Sex

An' it harm none, do what you will.
-THE WICCAN REDE

The Golden Rule: Do unto others as you
would have them do unto you.

DISCLAIMER

Some of us may feel that we have no problems with our sexuality. This essay
is not for you. Do your thing! Additionally, I would like to say that this section has been the hardest for me to write about of them all, but I feel that it
is important to say something despite its being so intensely personal a topic
for each one of us, and despite the fact that my own recovery in this area is
not as high as many other people. At the same time, I have decided to offer
my opinion on the topic as a starting ground for discussion. Please take this
content for what it's worth, a small comment, as is all the manuscript, in my
limited perspective.

A FEW COMMENTS

In early recovery, sexual issues can be overwhelming. It is also recommended that the whole problem be put on the back burner until after completing the Fourth Step. At the very least, we need to become mindful of our behavior so that we do not further behaviors which produce shame, guilt, and trauma in our lives. These behaviors can perpetuate the addictive process.

One of the problems with laying down sexual rules is that everyone has different standards. The precept, as I understand it, is about not causing harm through sexual behavior. That is a very personal matter. However, whatever we do, we should choose behaviors which do not harm us or anyone else. One way to do this is to suspend our sex life until we have a little more recovery. And this way we don't add to our Fourth Step in recovery.

When I was diagnosed with post-traumatic stress disorder in 1994, it was from a variety of very dysfunctional sexual experiences. Whether or not they can be categorized as sexual assault or date rape is beside the point; I was catatonic. During that period of time, I continued to put myself in situations where I was compromised sexually. It was not until I was institutionalized that I was safe. Even then, the trauma continued in my mind.

The Third Precept is about refraining from damaging sexual behavior. Many people find that as a result of their addiction, they have experienced things which are best left out of this manuscript. Everything ranging from being locked up in hotel rooms with pornos for days, to totally losing the desire for sex, or selling ourselves for drugs can result from being high on drugs, and addicted to drugs. How do we heal? Many of us who are mentally ill have a component to our disease which somehow links to our sexuality, and that can further complicate the process.

SOCIETY AND SEXUAL VIOLENCE

Deciding to refrain from harmful sexual behavior is something which we need to do as a society. The abuse of children, the frequent conjunction of sexual themes with violence, and the lack of respect for the integrity of the human person, especially women, have to cease. In recovery, we can draw a line that we will not allow ourselves to be abusive or be abused ever again, if it is within our power. We can take a stand against the violence in society by making a decision to honor both men and women for their sexuality and healthy ways.

I remember reading a news article that said that two-thirds of all women have been date raped. In *The Chalice and the Blade* by Riane Eisler, she states, "Some scholars estimate rapes now occur in the United States at the rate of one every 13 seconds."[1] Date rape can be defined as sexual interaction that continues after one of the participants has expressed an unwillingness to engage sexually. Date rape is characterized by being between people who are in some way acquainted with one another.

Now I'm going to say something which has empowered my healing process, and if it is not of benefit, totally disregard it. In the process of the Fourth Step, we explore our part in creating situations. Through doing a sexual inventory, I realize that I have a part to play in creating certain situations. Upon this realization, I discovered that these situations need not ever happen to me again. I didn't allow myself to be in compromising situations with people that I cannot trust, and because I was *no longer loaded*, I had the ability to monitor my surroundings the way that prevented these situations from ever happening again.

RECOVERING FROM CHILDHOOD SEXUAL ABUSE

A lot of people come into recovery with deep seated issues around sex that stem from childhood. The rate of children who have been molested is as high as 1 in 3. The widespread abuse of children is rampant and is connected to human trafficking, including the sex trade. Messages pervade the media that sexualize children, making it difficult to keep the mind clean of the disturbing trends towards eroticizing children instead of adults. It is apparent from the media and high-level convictions of child molesters and pedophile rings that the abuse of children reaches into the top levels of our society.

What is to be done? Self-compassion is a starting place. Toxic shame freezes people's ability to even think clearly about the topic. We all need to make it safe for people to exist where they are, wounded, harmed, trying to get our bearings. Often abuse engenders abuse, and people who have been the victims of abusive situations continue a cycle of violence. This in no way excuses the perpetration of sexual violence, but if we want to genuinely stop the problem, not just mouth disapproval in an ineffectual way, we need to commit to healing the cycle of violence at all the places where it arises.

---

1. Eisler, *The Chalice and the Blade*, 115.

A commitment to being a part of the solution is a necessary part of healing sexual violence. In our minds, and our consumption of media, and in our behavior, we need to commit and recommit to being a part of the solution. This is not about finger pointing and vigilante patrolling of people's behavior, although that may happen and be necessary and helpful. It is about committing to being healthy, honest, and positive in our sexual relationships.

CONSENT, CONTROL, AND COVERING

Normalizing and reinvigorating consensual sex between adults is an essential part of the process. Until men and women are encouraged and rewarded for healthy sexuality on a broader scale, this transformation will be slowed. We need to eroticize consent, and stop shaming, blaming, and judging sex in ourselves and others. Once healthy sex between adults becomes the standard, there will be fewer victims of abuse.

One of the ways I personally regained control over my ability to give and deny consent was by starting to wear hijab. In Islam, women are encouraged to wear a head scarf, and some people say it is a requirement of the religion. For me, I had no boundaries. I couldn't control my personal space and ended up making bad choices where I compromised my personal integrity because of it. When I was in the early stages of recovery from sexual assault, it was very hard for me to establish safety. My ability to be healthy around sex and love did not happen for me until I started wearing hijab. For women, head coverings were part of many religions, including Judaism and Christianity until very recently. Hijab is a choice that can help control personal space, so it is not easy for people to access women visually, or physically. There are modified versions of hijab too, like wearing a hat or a turban. You can drape a scarf around your neck. There is a boundary that keeps people with no boundaries safe at that point— you won't take off your hat or your clothes. This was a vital part of my recovery and changed my life for the better.

Men can also cover their heads to help guard their chastity. Chastity is not just a virtue for women. Many men feel out of control and want to stop being promiscuous. People can change their clothing to be more modest. In Islam, modesty is a big part of the religion. Guarding your chastity can be a source of spiritual strength and self-esteem, which is a big deal for those of us who have degraded ourselves over the years by being out of control and engaging in sex which we feel ashamed about.

CLEAN SEX

Having sex clean is a real challenge for some when drug use became an innate part of people's sexuality. My teacher, Imam Khorasani once told me, "We have all our holes for a reason and we are supposed to use them or they get sick. Our ears are for hearing, our nose is for breathing, our mouth is for eating, and our sex organs are there for a reason and we are supposed to use them." Being able to have clean consensual sex is a breakthrough for a lot of people where recovery begins to really feel doable.

Something that is essential to healthy sex is care of the body. Through exercise we can begin to detox places in our bodies where we have held abuse. Often this starts out as just walking in nature. Another great method for detoxing from toxic stress is saunas and just plain old baths. Taking a bath with a candle and bath salts can be tremendously healing, and open us up to the ability to connect in a relationship or partnership that helps us reach greater levels of self-actualization and awareness.

Diet is also a key element of being able to have sex clean. There are a number of healthy aphrodisiacs that can support positive sexual expression such as cocoa powder, fruits, kava, ashwagandha, and other supplements. Of course, all of this should be done in discussion with health care professionals in conjunction with individual needs, but exploring the options available through diet is a recovery-based choice that can really support people's ability to stay clean long term.

THE UPSIDE

Sex can be a wonderful way to explore our spirituality. Buddhism has a long tradition of sacred sex, going back into Hinduism and into the very beginnings of the human species. Sex can be a beautiful and healthy way to express ourselves and to interact with another human being. Of course, there is always the option of having sex with oneself, and that can be an act of self-love that can be very healing.

A lot of people think that just because we stopped using drugs, our sex lives have to end. A lot of us think that if we become spiritual, our sex lives definitely have to end. The precept on refraining from sexual irresponsibility doesn't mean we have to stop being sexual. It just means we have to avoid hurting ourselves and others in the process of expressing our very human, very natural sexuality. Shame and guilt derived from sex are not productive emotions. Guilt can be used, though, to see when we have compromised our principles, but wallowing in an endless self-incrimination, as many people do over the past, or simple masturbation, is not the point of this precept.

The problem with sex is that a lot of people use it to tune out life just like they used drugs. For addicts this can be very tempting. The key to working through all of this can be the Fourth and Fifth Steps. There we can do a sexual inventory and figure out what our values are, where we have compromised ourselves, where we do things that we feel good about. Based on that information, we can build a healthy sex life that doesn't feed our addiction and doesn't cause harm. Until that point, we can learn to be mindful of our sexuality and make sure that at the very least is not causing any harm.

MAKING FRIENDS WITH OUR BODIES

A crucial building block to healthy sexuality is to become comfortable with one's own body, or as the expression goes, "To dig the skin you're in." There are a lot of things that can help this happen, even in the midst of being really traumatized, or de-sensitized. You can stand in front of a mirror, and really look at yourself with love. This is a practice that Imam Khorasani taught me. He told me to stand in front of the mirror and tell myself that I love me, that I am special to me, that I am beautiful, and wonderful. I encourage all people to take time to do this. There is a certain thought that many people have that gazing in a mirror is vain, or self-centered. This is simply not the Islamic tradition. The Prophet (PBUH) carried a mirror and *kohl*, or a form of eyeliner, and a comb with him all the time. He, (PBUH), taught us to take care of ourselves. Brushing your teeth regularly can be a way to make friends with your body, and was heavily emphasized by the Prophet (PBUH). Also, regularly bathing, or showering, keeping your body clean, shaving, washing your hair, all these practices are central to the Islamic tradition and involve a high degree of self-love, self-care and friendship with the experience of being a person in a body.

Yes, we are spiritual beings, having the experience of being in a body, and there is a reason. The practices of the Islamic tradition support being in your body in a peaceful and harmonious way. It also includes not over-eating, and exercising. Our bodies are our temples, as the Bible says. We have a responsibility to take care of them, nurture them, and honor them. Until we have developed this practice, it is very difficult to engage with others in healthy ways around sex.

MINDFULNESS AND SEXUALITY

One of the first ways that we can become more mindful of our sexuality is taking inventory of what we have done and what we feel good about and do not feel good about. Most Twelve Step programs suggest that to fully appreciate this process, we need some time away from sex to be clear enough to assess any damage we have done to ourselves and others. Becoming mindful of our sexuality is a process which entails a lot of self-assessment and then action on the principles which we feel are right for us, then maintaining those principles in the same way that we learn to practice other principles such as open-mindedness and integrity. The first step in finding a way to be mindful about our sexuality requires that we are honest about what our spiritual values are, and then being honest about our highest goals to live according to those values. This process is different for each of us. One step toward being mindful is to watch our thoughts and to make a decision to let go of guilt, shame, and self-incrimination, the process of letting go which is entirely compatible with spirituality but not always compatible with some religious thought.

Homophobia for example, which we find in many religious traditions, is an act of judgment and hatred of the reality of some people's truth. Spirituality, on the other hand, teaches non-judgment and commitment to our own and others' integrity, thereby supporting the freedom of persons to love and to serve their spiritual calling. In an atmosphere of freedom and respect for others, we can all choose to follow our own path, usually a path from mind to heart. In finding this path, it is of utmost importance to let go of guilt, shame, and fear of judgment. Regardless of whom we are, we need to take time to affirm our highest calling to be present with ourselves and with those we choose to engage with sexually, regardless of whether we are gay, straight, bisexual, or whatever we are. In a culture full of messages about sex that are often conflicting and confusing, the first step is being mindful of cutting away the layers of attachment to our preoccupations with what we should be, or whom we were when we were loaded and get down to whom we really are. It is a lifelong process.

If we stop and look around, often we can identify some of the messages which we are being bombarded with, or that were placed upon us for the course of our lives. By letting all people exist in our presence, especially ourselves, and an attitude of non-judgment, we can begin the process of creating a world where all people are embraced for exactly who they are. And we can find the freedom to be ourselves by being mindful of some of the messages that we have received. When we are playing those tapes, in a way that oppresses us or anyone else, we can be mindful enough to set ourselves and those we meet free.

SEVEN TIMES A MINUTE

I read once that the average person thinks of sex seven times a minute. I think we all need to remember that there's more to life, and there's more to us, than whom we have sex with, how we had sex with them, how often we had sex with people, and how many people we had sex with.

Sex addiction is a real problem for a lot of people. This book is intended to convey my experience, and I am going to stay in the areas where I have expertise, so I am not going to share insights on sex and love addiction as it is something I do not know well. However, if you are struggling with staring at pornography for hours, or having unmanageable behaviors like compulsively seeking sex workers, serial fornication, speed dating, or other forms of sex that are destructive for you, it is important to address these behaviors, and often this requires seeing a qualified professional therapist. There are also groups like Sex and Love Addicts Anonymous (SLA) which can help, although I do not have personal experience and only know several people who have benefited. This is not intended as an endorsement or affiliation with SLA, only to be open about its existence, and to be clear that there is help for those seeking recovery.

Diagnosing addiction depends on many factors, but the major factor is that it interferes with the normal and healthy functioning of an individual. If anything is causing problems in sleep, family, work, normal recreational activities, healthy participation in social activities or community, or legal problems, then it is important to assess if it is a problem behavior and an addiction. Additionally, if you are trying to quit or reduce something because it is causing problems and you cannot, that is also a sign that something is an addiction. If these types of problems are presenting themselves in someone's sex life, sometimes people need to seek professional help. There is no shame in seeking help. That is why it is there.

TANTRA, RECOVERY, AND MARRIAGE

There is a lot of discussion in pop-culture of the subject of tantra, or sacred sex. The basic idea is that sex and desire can be a way to accelerate spiritual growth. The opening of the heart that is involved in simply smiling at someone you love is a step on the path to compassion. Basically, in my life my marriage has been a source of a lot of difficulty. Part of the challenge of making a marriage last is to continue to open your heart even when your partner has let you down. In the face of infidelity, or lies, or cheating, and other problems to open your heart and smile, to forgive, to recommit is a level up on the spiritual path. I am not preaching about condoning abuse, but it often occurs to me that maybe we should be less quick to split up marriages and families, and more willing to look deeply into our suffering, our anger, and our hurt, and open our hearts to the possibility that there are life lessons that come from commitment that cannot be learned as rapidly by breaking up our relationships. Sometimes a willingness to work through things, to smile, to continue to reconnect with what we love about our partners is an opportunity to deepen our compassion and appreciation of life in general.

RADICAL SELF-LOVE

Ultimately, we cannot draw water from an empty well. To love others, sexually, or otherwise, requires a commitment to love ourselves. Deciding when to commit and when to leave are decisions that hinge upon our best insights on ourselves. We are our own best experts on ourselves. Sharing with others about who we are and how we feel and think can give us clarity about this. Sometimes therapy can help this process. Sometimes couples therapy can also really help. Individual therapy is a starting place for finding answers to what we really want and seeking our own highest good. To really love ourselves, we have to know ourselves. There is a saying that God gave us three books from which to learn: Scripture, Nature, and ourselves. How do you love a book you have never read? We have to study ourselves to love ourselves, and the Fourth Step, taking inventory, is a crucial part of this, as is sharing this inventory with another human being.

Low-cost therapy is actually much more widely available than some people realize. There are often graduate schools that have low-cost sliding scale centers where interns are learning, and these centers can be a resource for fantastic low-cost help. Easy to find with a minimal amount of persistence and resourcefulness, investing extra time in personal development is something that we can all benefit from, and something that we all deserve.

MINDFUL SELF-CARE

Part of having a healthy sex life is having a healthy relationship to one's own body and mindfulness can help this. Mindfully brushing teeth, using dental floss or mouthwash, washing the face, or dressing in clean clothes can all be a way to take care of oneself mindfully. Exercise and movement can be important parts of mindful self-care as well. Please take my teacher's instruction and look in the mirror and tell yourself how beautiful you are. One wonderful way to practice mindful self-care is to take a bath, using plain table salt, or Epsom salt, or bath salts. Salt baths clear one's aura and can help in relaxing and calming trauma in the nervous system. Taking good care of oneself, practicing loving self-care is a form of loving the gift of life, and an expression of peace and gratitude that can make the world, and sex, safer, happier, and more peaceful.

Chapter Seven

The Fifth Step

And with Him are the keys of the unseen; none knows them except Him. And He knows what is on the land and in the sea. Not a leaf falls but that He knows it. And no grain is there within the darknesses of the earth and no moist or dry but that it is written in a Clear Book.
-QURAN 6: 59

Fifth Step Prayer: Oh Ever-living and Ever-lasting, I beg you for your mercy. Rectify all my affairs and don't leave me alone even for the blink of an eye.

THE FIFTH STEP STATES, "We admitted to God, to ourselves and to another human being the exact nature of our wrongs." Talking about and speaking about the ways in which I have wronged myself and others is itself a process of clarification. Some things are true as they are, and it's final, and other truths can be somewhat of a moving target. This is not to cop out of being honest or rigorous in looking at reality, but sometimes, in particular, something can feel like a really big deal and then with time, it seems like, wow that wasn't all that important. The Fifth Step is an opportunity to be honest and open, and to have another human being give more perspective to the storyline that I have in my head about things in ways that make my perceptions more accurate. I remember once, I thought this wasn't such a big deal, and my sponsor was like, "Wow that's messed up," and I had more of a conscience about it. And then there have been times when I was wracked with guilt and shame, and my sponsor has said "Really you don't need to get hung up on that so much." And I let go of a lot of the emotional baggage that I was carrying. Having another set of eyes on things has the ability to change the reality of something in my head. This is part of why being able to trust a sponsor is so important, because they have a lot of power to influence the way I see myself and the world.

Facing who we are is an act of courage, including being willing to walk through the discomfort that it can bring up. It calls for reliance on God. When our emotional resources dwindle, and our stress and pain increase, there is a point at which we no longer choose to open our hearts but choose to shut down, act out, and often anger, self-hate, and despair are the places that we go with the pain. The Fifth Step is a way to practice opening the heart in the midst of pain. By letting off some of the pressure about life, it gives us practice in being present and vulnerable with another human being, and clears the way for relationships to improve

HONEST, OPEN MINDED, WILLING AND HUMBLE

As recovery progresses, when we behave in patterns that no longer support recovery principles, we are usually growing enough to feel that old habits are no longer spiritually comfortable. The old saying that the road gets narrower is so true. What was tolerable in our interpersonal relationships 20 or 10 or even 5 years ago doesn't feel comfortable any more. We look at our past honestly, we think with an open mind about our mistakes, and we choose to be willing to change. This takes humility.

The old saying the elbow does not bend backward is true here. We have to submit to the rules and boundaries as they appear and not worry too much about what we see as what should happen or should be said or should be felt or thought, but just what is, given people the right to being who they actually are.

THE INTEGRATED SELF AND NEW INTEGRITY

Integration and integrity are connected to the same root word. The process of bringing together our past in a coherent inventory that we share with another human being opens the doors to a renewed integrity for most people who go through the process. Understanding ourselves allows us to gain an understanding of the many parts of ourselves, and bring them together into a coherent whole. This process of integration is the foundation of a new integrity.

AWARENESS

One of the major gifts of recovery, both from mental illness and addiction, is the ability to better understand ourselves and our lives. Often the fog has been so thick that we do not see our own motives for our behaviors clearly. For myself, there are places in my life that I looked back on, before I got clean as well as after, and I could see clear motives in retrospect that I was unaware of at the time. This is not to say to indulge in the attribution of negative motives to our choices as people can sometimes do. It's not to say, "Oh I was just using that person," or didn't care about what I said or what I did at the time about someone or something, as can be tempting to do when we engage in self-reflection from a negative view of ourselves. Our motives are usually a mix of higher emotions and intentions such as love and care and good goals, and lower motives such as avoiding pain, manipulation, and dishonest exploitation and abuses of personal power.

When I listen to people who are really spiritual talk about themselves, they tend to have insight into their motives that other people lack. This is in a sense a connection to the secret heart of ourselves that is the Divine, the shiny mirror of the soul. The process of the Fifth Step is a way to shine in the mirror of the soul so that we can see it more clearly. This process of clearing away the wreckage and debris so that we see our hearts better, and so that our hearts see better, is tremendously liberating and requires insight, mindfulness, and reflection. Sharing the process with another human being deepens the insights we gain

LIVING A NEW WAY OF LIFE

Changing our behaviors is a consequence of understanding what we have done, and our part in our mistakes. There is a common thread in a lot of discourses about power and relationships that looks for victimization as a way to deal with uncomfortable facts of bad choices. The Quran deals with this idea in a way that is so direct it clearly shows this idea of blaming other people's power for our mistakes is an ancient and time-honored way to cop out of responsibility. In the Quran there is a recurring theme of how God will address people and call them to account, and they will blame the strong for their errors, and then the strong will say, "Well it wasn't actually our fault," and God will, sadly, damn both the strong and the weak. The Quran clearly teaches that blaming others is not going to be an option when we are called to account.

In taking the Fifth Step we choose to look at our part in our mistakes and the pain we have caused others straight in the face, both to ourselves, to God and to another human being, and own our part. This is tremendously freeing because it is empowering us to be responsible for ourselves. Unfortunately, in addiction, people often have chosen to avoid taking responsibility, and this is a direct and proactive cure for that diseased thinking and behavior.

Looking at our mistakes, and our part in making them, naturally opens the door to thinking about how we can live better, more productive, and positive lives when we contribute to the happiness of our loved ones and communities, not their suffering. The input of a sponsor helps clarify this process by bringing light to our Fourth Step and providing insights into our choices.

SECRETS

One of the beautiful things about the Fifth Step is that we can finally stop hiding our secrets. Many of us have lived with intense shame about things that we have done or thought or said that haunts us on a daily basis. The process of sharing our inventory involves letting someone know our secrets. We let our sponsor, and God, see us, and we get the relief of being accepted when someone knows us. The old saying, "We are as sick as our secrets" is true. The act of sharing our stories with another human being allows us to let go of the pain, shame, and guilt, and get some relief, sometimes, for the first time in our lives.

INTIMACY AND SPONSORSHIP

Intimacy is something that is a central part of the Sufi path in the form of the relationship to the *shayk* or teacher, in traditional forms of the religion. The reason for needing a guide on the path is complicated, and multifaceted in the historical context, but modernity has further complicated it with the difficulty of connecting to teachers, in spite of good intentions to join a spiritual community. The idea of a guide contains both the idea that the light we seek in spirituality and connection is not easy to access and, thus, just contact will help but also the idea that the route is complicated, and someone is needed who knows the path.[1]

One of the beauties of sponsorship in the Twelve Step fellowships is that this need for a guide is built into the program. A critical advantage of sponsorship, in addition to the value of guidance through the steps, is that it provides one of the first major opportunities to experience intimacy that many addicts have ever had. In addiction, many people find themselves disconnected from the rest of humanity and from themselves. The experience of getting clean can be very raw, with emotions surfacing that many addicts have never felt. The advantage of sponsorship is that it provides a space to experience these emotions in relationship to another human being, and develop the ability to connect, trust, and experience being seen and heard in a unique and transformative way.

In my own relationship with my teacher of Sufism, I spent many hours talking with him and having lunch with him. It was a process of being accepted and loved. I had esteem for him, and the fact that he valued me gave me a sense of self-worth. Likewise, a sponsor's investment in us as people can give us a sense of personal value that opens doors to the ability to face truths about ourselves that are too raw to comprehend when we are feeling rejected and hated, as many of us feel in addiction, mental illness, or even in life in general.

Similarly, the women who have sponsored me have given me a sense of my personal value that has transformed me. The old saying in Twelve Step rooms, "We will love you until you love yourself" has been overwhelmingly true for me. It was true for me in recovery from addiction, it was true for

1. Hammerle, Ali, Newman, and Pryor, *Sufi Grace*, 38-43.

me in recovery from mental illness with therapists and psychiatrists, and it was true for me in the Muslim community. Being loved unconditionally allows us to love ourselves and life in a unique way.

The experience of sharing a Fifth Step is a vital part of this process in that it is a moment in time when we share our deepest truths, mistakes, and pain with another human being, and they see us. As the saying goes, "Into-me-you-see" is another way to write intimacy.

PART THREE

Steps Six Through Nine
and Refinement of Character

Chapter Eight

Steps Six and Seven

> Call yourselves to account before you are called to account, and
> weigh yourselves before you are weighed.
> -Umar ibn Al-Khattab

The Sixth Step states, "We became entirely willing to have God remove all these defects of character." The Seventh Step goes right along with the Sixth Step. In the Seventh Step, we ask our Higher Power or look to our spiritual roots to stop acting out on our character defects. The Seventh Step states, "We humbly ask Him to remove our shortcomings." Here are some approaches to the Sixth and Seventh Steps.

TIME

When we look at Steps Six and Seven, we are involved in a process which takes a lot of time, usually the rest of our lives. We perceive time is flowing from the past to the present moment to the future. We perceive time as absolute as well. It seems like time just is, always the same, always flowing evenly. This perception of time has remained the same in Western culture for centuries. Linear perceptions of time give birth to ideas such as progress, evolution, and economic development in the third world. Unfortunately, this idea of time is outdated.

Time, said Einstein, is relative. The reality is that we each carry our own internal clock, and the clock runs differently depending on gravity, and the speedway traveling, which affects gravity (the old e=mc2). If you place a clock on the earth and a clock on a very high tower, the two clocks run at different rates because the gravity of the earth decreases as you move away from the surface of the planet.[1]

Additionally, at the quantum level, time moves in both forward and backward dimensions. Time at the quantum level loses all meaning. A nuclear physicist named Heisenberg discovered the fact that you cannot measure both the location and the velocity of a subatomic particle. If you measure velocity, you change the location, and to locate the location, you change the velocity. The closer you come to an accurate measure of one, the less accurate becomes your measurement of the other. The renowned physicist Stephen Hawking says in *A Brief History of Time*,

> The uncertainty principle had profound implications for the way in which we view the world. Even after more than 70 years they have not been fully appreciated by many philosophers, and are still the subject of much controversy. The uncertainty principle signaled an end to LaPlace's dream of the theory of science, a model of the universe that would be completely deterministic: one certainly cannot predict future events exactly if one cannot accurately measure the present state of the universe precisely.[2]

Pierre La Place took Newton's laws of physics and came up with the theory of scientific determinism. With the clockwork idea, he went so far as to say that not only were there rules that govern the universe, these laws also govern human behavior.[3] Well, this model, as Stephen Hawking says, just doesn't work. At the quantum level, not only are things totally uncertain and merely waves of probability as far as we know, time seems not to affect things at the quantum level. To illustrate, a round black hole's particles travel into the past and back again on a microscopic level. Stephen Hawking has concluded, "Radiation by black holes shows that quantum theory allows for travel back in time on a microscopic level and that such time

1. Davies, *God and the New Physics*, 122.

2. Hawkings, *Brief History of Time*, 57.

3. Hawkings, *Brief History of Time*, 55.

travel produces observable effects."[4] It is because of quantum time realities, or the lack thereof, and the relativity principle that people are beginning to think that time travel might be possible. So where are the past, present and future then? If this interests you, Stephen Hawking's book *A Brief History of Time* is the best reference that I have found for lay people on the subject of time.

TIME AND THE GODDESS

There are some cultures that perceive time as cyclical. In Paleolithic and Neolithic cultures, we are almost certain that our Goddess worshiping ancestors saw the time like a wheel which turned around and around repeating itself. Birth, life, death, and rebirth were seen to be like the cycles of the Moon, ever repeating themselves.

Anne Baring and Jules Cashford have stated in their text *The Myth of the Goddess* that the moon served as a great symbol of the Goddess:

> (She was) the Unifying power of the Mother of all. She was the measure of the cycle of time, and of celestial and earthly connection and influence. She governed the fecundity of women, the waters of the sea and all phases of increase and decrease. The seasons followed each other in sequence as the faces of the moon followed each other. She was an enduring image, both of renewal in time and over timeless totality, because what was apparently lost with the waning moon was restored with the waxing moon. Duality, imaged as the waxing and waning moon, was contained and transcended in her totality. So, analogously, life and death did not have to be perceived as opposites, but could be seen in succeeding each other in a rhythm that was endless. [5]

TIME AND CHARACTER DEFECTS

The Sixth and Seventh steps are easier when you don't take time so seriously. We can get very caught up in our self-improvement projects. We become very aggressive towards ourselves. Using the analogy of the United States imposed early on in its history—we must manifest our destiny and plow from sea to sea, conquering territory to be truly great. If we look at

4. Hawkings, *Brief History of Time,* 169.
5. Baring and Cashford, *Myth of the Goddess,* 21.

time as relative or cyclical, we can see that a "conquer and destroy" model for approaching character defects as fast as possible is based on a limited understanding of reality. There is another approach.

If we wake up to who we fundamentally are, we can learn to watch ourselves change from moment to moment. Sometimes we are really greedy. We want all the best friends, the nicest cars, the best clothes. Sometimes we're really insecure; we are really worried about what everyone is thinking about us. We are sure that we have a booger hanging out of our noses, and we're too afraid to stick a finger up there and find out because someone might be watching. The willingness to observe ourselves in these moments of difficulty can be a great way to observe how impermanent our character defects actually are. When I say impermanent, I mean that we're not greedy all of the time, nor are we insecure all of the time. We don't have to get caught up in our "we will be good" projects.

The Seventh Step is inherently humbling when we take this approach. Things come and go, just like the seasons, just like civilizations, just like the 1980s. If we think we have a character defect that is as permanent as Rome, we can be relieved by this attitude. And sometimes we think that a character defect is gone, like when we think winter really has left, and then along comes the storm from Alaska. If we watch ourselves and try to be present to our own juicy, squishy, crazy selves, we can lighten up a lot. Character defects can be the source of a great awakening. There is a story about a woman who went to a Yogi and said, "Yogi, I want to become enlightened and live every moment fully awake." The Yogi set a demon on her who chased her around for the rest of her life whacking her over the head with a stick yelling, "Now! Now!" Character defects can be like that in the sense that they keep us in the present moment just as the demon with the stick did for the woman getting hit. Waking up to it all can be painful, but it certainly makes us present.

THE FALSE SELF AND THE TRUE SELF

Possibly, this perspective that character defects are cyclical, and the self-purification that I have spoken about, the quest for self-knowledge, should not be a self-improvement project seems like a contradiction. However, the idea is that the process of self-purification, and working on our defects of character should have a quality of self-acceptance and self-forgiveness, and not aggression. It is based on self-love, both in recovery and Sufism.

There are several ways to see the idea of purifying yourself from your character defects, including understanding and elevating the true self instead of the false self. If the true self is a reflection of the Divine, then our egos are like veils over our true nature which is more pure and good.

Another way to see the process of clearing away our character defects involves the metaphor of cleaning the soul like a mirror so that it can reflect the light of the divine.

Both of these approaches do involve a more progressive and negative view of character defects than just viewing them as waves in the ocean of being, but it is important to keep in mind that the Sufi perspective on the self is that our true nature is good, and refining the self is not an aggression against ourselves, but the work of revealing our true selves. We are all born good, according to Islam, and life makes us deviate from that original good nature or *fitra*. The process of recovery is a return to our *fitra*. It is easier when we understand that our character defects, and our old habits, our lusts, and delusions, are not our true self, to have faith and work to elevate our character. These character defects are not who we really are. Faith that it is a process that is God guided helps, too. God did not bring us this far to abandon us.

It is important to think about what we are creating with our deeds and our habits. The Quran states, "O you who have believed, fear Allah. And let every soul look to what it has put forth for tomorrow—and fear Allah. Indeed, Allah is Acquainted with what you do. And be not like those who forgot Allah, so He made them forget themselves." (Quran 59: 18-19) We need to remember to take account of ourselves.

REPENTANCE

The idea of repentance in Sufism is a central pillar. Also known as *tauba*, the concept of repentance is about the refining of the self. Fear of hell, as a place or a mind state, and a desire for peace, as a final resting place, or a state of being in the world, is traditionally, in both Buddhism and Islam, the basis for repentance. In Sufism it also has to do with closeness to God in the sense of clearing away the confusion and wreckage caused by the false self. Repentance begins in the first three steps with the decision to live a better way of life. It continues in personal inventory in Steps Four through Seven.

Repentance in Sufism means to renounce everything that is not godly, and in a sense everything in the self that is not God.[6] Dr. Angha writes, "Repentance literally means 'to turn away' and that is the turning back from an inferior state towards a superior state."[7] *Tauba* takes many forms, and in Islam, *tauba* has been connected to mindfulness with *dhikr*, or the remembrance of the names of God. There are many ways to do this but the simplest one is an Arabic phrase, *Astaghfirullah*. It means, "God forgive me." Repeating this and meditating on our mistakes is a practice that I have engaged in extensively, and it has helped me to no end. It is like a karmic house cleaning, and needs to be done regularly on the spiritual path.

One of the beautiful truths of the Sufi path is that the Prophet (PBUH), the perfect person, repented extensively in spite of having no sins. This is an example to the believers, and to us as addicts. It isn't a sign of weakness to repent, or to ask God for forgiveness. Abd al-Qadir al-Jilani describes how the Prophet (PBUH), in spite of his perfection, was instructed by God to repent 100 times a day. He says, "He set the pure Prophet as an example of how to repent— by begging Allah to erase one's ego, one's personality, one's individuality, all of oneself. . .that is true repentance."[8] The Quran states that God forgives our mistakes, but that we have to engage in the process of repentance. (Quran 39: 53-56) The process of working on our character defects, and of becoming willing to change is an essential part of the Twelve Steps, and of religion.

One of the things that is hard with mental illness is to keep looking at yourself when family members, doctors, or friends, call you out about your mental health challenges. It is easy to be defensive. It is easy to decide to stop taking medications, and to relapse into poor mental health. Sometimes it feels really aggressive when doctors ask us about "our voices," or our family and friends withdraw from us or ask us to get help. One way to avoid this is to be vigilant about taking care of our mental health ourselves. Taking responsibility for our mental health is an act of courage. Being willing to seek help, proactively, from doctors, take medications, pursue therapy and meetings, and realistically assess how we are doing is part of the process of recovery. It gets easier as it becomes a habit, but when we first get diagnosed it is often painfully difficult. I have been taking medication for almost 30

6. al-Qadir al-Jilani, *Secret of Secrets*, 35.

7. Angha, *Principles of Sufism*, 29.

8. al-Qadir al-Jilani, *Secret of Secrets*, 35.

years, and it was a long process to get to the point where I appreciated the blessing of having medication to help me

BECOMING WILLING TO HAVE GOD REMOVE OUR DEFECTS OF CHARACTER

One of the important things to understand about the Sixth and Seventh Steps is that we are asking God to do this work for us. While we have to know what to ask for, this does not mean we ourselves are doing the work of the change in our character. Giving up our bad habits is often very difficult. But this process is guided by a loving higher power. This brings to mind the famous story about how God called upon the Prophet Ibrahim to sacrifice his son. Prophet Ibrahim was told by God to sacrifice his only son, and being the obedient believer, he went to obey God. He took his son, built an altar, laid his son on the altar and prepared to sacrifice him. Sheikh Muzaffar relates:

> As he raised his sacrificial knife God said to the angels, 'Look at the faith and love of my friend, Abraham. He is even willing to sacrifice his only son in obedience to my commands.' Then Abraham attempted to cut his son's throat with the razor-sharp sacrificial knife. Nothing happened. There was not even a scratch on Ismail. Abraham tried again with the same result. He tried a third time but still the knife would not cut. Then, Abraham struck a nearby rock with the knife. The blade split the rock in two. God gave speech to the knife blade. 'You see Abraham, only God's will enables knives to cut, fire to burn, and water to drown. Unless God permits I can cut nothing. And if God wills I can even split stone.' . . . God demands sacrifices of all those who would know their Lord. We are asked to sacrifice for God's sake what we often love best- our attachments to the world, our bad habits, our arrogance. The great lovers of God have often found that once they have been willing to give up anything other than God, they received everything- material as well as spiritual abundance.[9]

The work of self-transformation does not happen through extreme self-will, although a force of will is involved. Ultimately, the act of changing our bad habits is about opening a way for God to transform our lives. We ask for help, we become willing, and God takes over.

9. Ozak, *Love is the Wine*, 61-62.

MINDFULNESS AND CHARACTER DEFECTS

Become aware of some of your best and worst elements of character. Ask yourself if you were acting spiritually or not. Become aware of the craving to act out on your better thoughts, and the craving to stay in unhealthy patterns. This process of changing towards a more spiritual life is similar to redirecting rivers. At first, it takes a lot of work to redirect the flow, but then the river begins to flow naturally in a new channel. Take the time and effort to recognize the flow of your thoughts, words, and actions. Become mindful of your spiritual health from day one today by noticing your character defects.

My sponsor says that when we are acting on a character defect, we come up short spiritually. That is why in Step Seven we don't ask for a change in our character defects; instead, we ask for the removal of our shortcomings. The next time you feel a character defect manifesting in you, remind yourself to be mindful of your actions. Often this is enough to prevent coming up short spiritually.

For me, I am coming up short spiritually, as well, when I act out on my mental difference in a way which negatively affects me or anyone else. Be mindful of the effect your mental difference has on you, and try to apply the spiritual principles that your sponsor is teaching you to the challenges of your mental difference. For example, when I am hallucinating and someone is talking to me, I say, "Hallucinating," and try to come back to be present enough to hear the person who's talking to me. This is innately more respectful.

Chapter Nine

Steps Eight and Nine

> Forgive us our debts as we forgive our debtors.
> -THE LORD'S PRAYER

STEPS EIGHT AND NINE involve healing the wounds that we have inflicted on others and ourselves through our self-centeredness or other defects that we deal with in Steps Six and Seven. It is important to work Steps Six and Seven first so that we know that we are going to hurt somebody doing the same thing we just made amends for. Step Eight says, "We made a list of all persons we have harmed and became willing to make amends to them all." Step Nine says, "We made direct amends wherever possible except when to do so would injure them or others." Steps Eight and Nine then are about cleaning up the mess we made by being actively practicing alcoholics, addicts, or whatever addiction we have been practicing.

THE TRUTH ABOUT KARMA

Amends are really about improving our karma. But what does this mean? The use of the word karma is widespread in the United States. While the way it is used has a colloquial meaning, the true teaching about karma is slightly different. The commonly held notion of karma is the "what goes around comes around mentality," but this is not an accurate interpretation of what the Buddha taught. The Buddha taught that there was a 12-part cycle to life. That which is expressed in the cycles of existence of beings was called dependent arising, although dependent arising came to have broader meanings over the lengthy development of Buddhist philosophy. But in the case of the cycles of the existence of beings, there were 12 stages of the Buddha. The first three were ignorance, action, and consciousness. Action is translated from the word karma. We have already talked about the self-mistake. If we do not even have a self to call our own, how do we work to accumulate status and wealth? We are all part of what was once called Indra's web, the vibrating fields of quantum possibility.

The Buddha taught that there were only aggregates which made up the human person. This teaching was in sharp contrast to the teachings of Hinduism which taught the doctrine of *atman*, or soul. *Atman* was considered to be one permanent immortal soul which moved from one body to the next until the time of enlightenment. Because *atman* was permanent, and carried with it all the traces of former existences, you had to work your way up to achieve enlightenment. Normal people had too much past life baggage for enlightenment to occur. It was assumed that if they were in the lower castes to be able to attain freedom from the cycles of birth and death, they had to first be born into a higher caste, a gradual process which took lifetimes. They had too much coming around in terms of bad karma.

The Buddha, on the other hand, taught that the ignorance regarding the insubstantiality of the self leads to misguided actions, these actions lead to a confused consciousness which in turn, down the line, causes clinging and more suffering. Actions were evaluated as the way in which consciousness was created. Your karma, the weight of your actions, wasn't like a bank that you stored up savings in for good things, or wrote checks on when you did bad things. The relative ignorance or wisdom of a combination of the five aggregates lead to relatively enlightened or unenlightened actions, and this in turn has an effect on your consciousness.[1] It isn't about getting lots of good stuff for our good deeds; we just see that we have done the right thing and knowing the action is pure, are happy in our consciousness.

Because anyone at any time could wake up to the fundamental non-solidity of self, the actions change and become pure and, then, so could their consciousness. The Buddha taught that anyone can wake up and reach

---

1. Anonymous, *Dhammapada*, 109.

enlightenment. They just had to understand the fundamental nature of reality. This is very good news for addicts because it means that we don't have to be running away from the huge weight of past history. As the saying goes, "You're not responsible for your disease, but you are responsible for your recovery." We don't have to carry around everything we did in our disease like it's going to damn us to some awful hell someday. We can wake up at any time.

SEPTEMBER 11TH AND KARMA

In the tragedy of September 11, many people thought it was karma coming back to the United States for all the things that our government has done wrong. But if that was so, why were those people victims of 9/11? Was it their karma but they died in the attack? Why did they pay for the actions of our government? That doesn't seem to make any sense. In fact, karma doesn't lead to either good outcomes or to punishment. It proceeds from a right understanding of the self and produces a clear happy mind, not lots of good luck. The karma of the victims of the attack produced their consciousness at the time of death, and that in turn dictated their feelings as a result. I heard about the man who stayed in a tower with his friend in a wheelchair because he didn't want to leave his friend alone. Their consciousness must've been very clear and bright at the time of their death they had such a strong friendship.

KARMA AND AMENDS

When making amends, often we build up a feeling that we have done a bunch of good stuff, so the world now owes us. We think if we just fix what we've done wrong, our lives will improve. But this is not the case. It is our perspective on our lives that improves. If we go into our amends thinking that we are putting a bunch of money in the bank to get a lot of success and prestige and green lights and parking spaces, we are not understanding the process. Even if we expect people to congratulate us, or forgive us, we may be disappointed. Sometimes, we even have to go to jail or prison as a result of amends. However, we act out of knowing that in attempting to heal others, we heal ourselves, because we are all connected. Through that healing, we become happier people, less afraid of our own shadow. That's our wisdom, leading to our karma, the amends, which then produce a happier state for your consciousness.

LOVING KINDNESS AND STEP EIGHT

Really wishing the best for other people is also at the heart of the Eighth Step. In our self-obsession, often we justify behavior that we see as necessary to satisfy our lust for power, property, or prestige. This type of hate, you could argue, is bad because it is not in our self-interest because "what goes around comes around," and for every action there is an equal and opposite reaction. How is it true if good karma isn't a guarantee of a happy life? Well, let's be real. In the Judeo-Christian-Islamic tradition, we're all clear, we believe in hell. But, if this news scares a bit, the Buddha actually believed in hell and taught about hell as well. And contrary to watered down, New Age versions where "it's all just a state of mind," I believe, people actually reappear at some point in a real place that is very bad if they don't do anything to correct their mistakes.

But honestly, that isn't at the core of the Eighth and Ninth Step. The Twelve Step program is about being less selfish, and self-obsessed, about being good people, and contributing to society, not robbing, cheating and stealing. The idea of loving kindness, or really genuinely caring about people is a central teaching in many Buddhist communities. Honestly, caring about people is the right thing to do regardless, because kindness is a spiritual principle. Yes, it takes you out of hell in your mind, fear or getting caught, shame and guilt for hurting people (if you have a conscience), worrying about ethics, but it also feels good to care. You know, some people have a glow in their face. Everyone loves them. That is usually connected to them being loving nice people. That is the state of mind of heaven.

Back to an earlier discussion, the Gnostics believed that the soul, upon death, would go in the direction that it was cultivated. If it was cultivated towards earthly passions, greed, lust for power and prestige, it would sink into a bad state upon death. If it was cultivated towards love, and care, towards longing for truth and righteousness, it would launch itself towards heaven, floating up into the higher elevations of the spirit.

Loving kindness meditations help cultivate this type of bright light in the soul. Making amends is an action version of loving kindness meditation, where we in concrete ways tell people we care that we have hurt them.

FORGIVENESS

Part of the challenge of Step Eight is the challenge of forgiving people with whom we have a mixed past, including ourselves. Sometimes we have harmed people who have also harmed us. Sometimes, we have harmed ourselves. The old saying is that most people should put themselves first on their amends list, and this means that part of Step Eight is forgiving ourselves.

The Islamic tradition comments a lot about forgiveness, including forgiveness from God, as well as many instructions about forgiving others. The Quran states, "Hold to forgiveness" (Quran 9: 199) and the saint Abd al-Qadir al-Jilani states, "To forgive is the greatest sign of the believer."[2] The Quran also tells the believer, "And not equal are the good deed and the bad. Repel evil by that which is better; and thereupon the one whom between you and him is enmity will become as though he was a devoted friend." (Quran 41: 34) and again "Repel evil with good." (Quran 23: 96)

Another famous story is that of the necklace where Aisha, one of the wives of the Prophet (PBUH), lost a necklace and was delayed behind the caravan of the Prophet (PBUH). When she caught up to the rest of the people, she was accused of not having guarded her chastity by malicious gossipers. God sent down a verse to the Prophet (PBUH) which cleared her of any wrongdoing and chastised the gossipers. Simultaneously, her father, Abu Bakr decided never to forgive people who were involved in the slander. Then Allah sent down the famous verse telling Abu Bakr to forgive, saying, "Pardon and forgive. Don't you love that Allah should forgive you?" (Quran 24: 22)

REPENTANCE

Tauba is an important part of Steps Eight and Nine because it prevents us from continuing to make the same mistakes. As stated in the previous chapter on Steps Six and Seven, *tauba* is a pillar in the Sufi path and a central part of the Twelve Steps.

---

2. al-Qadir al-Jilani, *Secret of Secrets*, 63.

CONSCIENCE

The process of deciding to turn away from oppression and exploiting others sounds praiseworthy to almost everyone. This is because we all have in us the capacity, as mere veils over the Divine, to hear this call to genuine presence with the Other through mercy. Kabir Helminski, in *Living Presence* states, "The purpose of life from the Sufi perspective is to attain communion with the Divine, to know and experience the true dimensions of divine beauty, intelligence, and Love."[3] Our conscience is like a radar system that allows us to navigate life towards our true goal with our true purpose as the guiding light. *Tauba* attunes our conscience to enable us to see this radar screen, so we can avoid making mistakes. Step Eight and Nine involve the fruition of a mind state built from the previous steps and allow us to clear the wreckage of the past and begin to build, navigate, and live more freely and fully.

Helminski talks about how this experience of conscience contradicts the false self. The false self, based on ego, vanity, self-centered fear, self-obsession, is derived from lack of understanding of reality, as well as the inherited flaws of society. Helminski states, "Human beings will inevitably face experiences of suffering and disappointment that break down some of the features of the false self and give rise to moments of true remorse and essential empathy."[4] This process is key to recovery. The process entails where we come face to face with the limits of the false self, and realize in our hearts that it is in conflict with our true purpose, and our true self.

LIVING AMENDS

One of the most important things we can do to make amends to our loved ones is to change the way we live. In this sense, as soon as we get clean, we have started to make amends. The ongoing process of becoming better people, and not repeating the damage we have done through our selfishness or neglect, is one of the most important things we can do to help our loved ones heal. It is not possible to heal the damage of years of bad behavior with a simple apology. Often, we have broken people's hearts, traumatized them, caused them extreme suffering. The best way to apologize for this type of

---

3. Helminski, *Living Presence*, 81.
4. Helminski, *Living Presence*, 83.

long-term damage is to change the way we live. We can take comfort in the fact that we have started this process by getting clean.

A lot of us who suffer from mental illness have done something else which has caused our families a lot of harm. When we got sick with mental illness, a lot of us had a moment when we were told we could benefit from medication, and we might have started meds only to stop taking them and become sick again. When we stopped taking our meds, and became mentally sick again, losing our jobs, making insane choices, wreaking havoc in our lives and hurting our families and friends, we caused serious harm. The decision to discipline ourselves to take medicine that we need is a living amends we can make in the face of the suffering we have caused our families with our self-will and self-neglect.

If we make the decision to change our medication, it should always be under the care of a competent psychiatrist who is monitoring our medications and our mental health, not simply stopping our medication without proper supervision. Deciding to change meds is a big decision, and requires the input of a qualified doctor. I have changed my meds many times over the years, sometimes on my own without the care of a doctor, and sometimes with the care of a doctor. It has always gone better under the care of a psychiatrist than it has when I have cold turkey quit medication because I thought I was cured.

A lot of times, people diagnosed with mental illness can recover and stop taking medication, and a lot of times people need medication for the rest of their lives. Mental illness, like high blood pressure, or type 2 diabetes is a chronic relapsing condition that will come back in people if the conditions become present or if sufficient health isn't restored. The shame is not in taking meds for our health, it is in neglecting our health through delusions that we are cured when we still need help.

AMENDS TO SOCIETY

Another type of living amends is amends to society. Each of us has damaged our communities in unique ways. Some of us have stolen, or abused people, even killed people. Some of us have been the first people to help other people get high and watched them go on to suffer from addiction themselves. Some of us have neglected our children, or parents. All kinds of damage to society have resulted from our diseases. Part of making amends is changing from a toxic bad influence on society, to a productive member of society. This looks different for different people. Some of us volunteer, some engage in community organizing or march for civil rights, or simply do service in myriad big and small ways. The important part of making amends to society is to make sure that we are taking some kind of action to contribute positively to the world, when before we were a liability to our communities.

AMENDS TO OURSELVES

For many of us, when we get to recovery, the person who has done us the most damage is us. Sponsors often say to put yourself first on your amends list. Choices where we have abandoned our well-being, neglected our health, put ourselves in harm's way, chosen to take the wrong risks, not take risks, or the countless other ways we have let ourselves down weigh heavy on most of us in recovery, especially early recovery. We may have broken our children's hearts in some way, and we can't forgive ourselves, or hurt friends or family. Forgiving ourselves is important, and letting go of our resentments against ourselves, and also taking care of ourselves going forward with better choices, where we respect and honor ourselves is an important form of amends.

MINDFULNESS AND KARMA

It is important that we work the steps in order. We should not make any amends until we have worked through the previous steps. At the same time, we can become mindful of doing good actions rather than continuing to create situations which bring a mess of guilt and shame, or cause more suffering in the world. Go through your day noticing your actions. At the end of the day, write down what you did that was good for your world and others around you and what was destructive. Begin to be mindful enough to do one good deed during the day, and then tell nobody about it. That will immediately brighten your consciousness. It could be as simple as emptying an ashtray. Anything will do. It takes a bit of attention to notice something everyone else is avoiding sometimes. And that takes mindfulness.

PART FOUR

The Steps of Ongoing Maintenance

Chapter Ten

Setbacks and Relapse

THE TENTH STEP STATES, "We continued to take personal inventory and when we were wrong promptly admitted it." The Tenth Step is the daily maintenance step. There are a number of ways to work the Tenth Step, but let's look at one thing the Tenth Step focuses on, relapse prevention. Mental illness and drug addiction are progressive and chronic illnesses. As such, they tend to recur in times of stress, and stress can come at any moment. There is a direct correlation between stress in the occurrence of schizophrenia. The more stress, the more psychosis. I experienced a major relapse into paranoia over waiting to hear from grad school, and spent a long time dealing with the aftershocks. I recovered through intensive therapy, increased medication, and a lot of other work. Other people may experience their own symptoms recurring at higher levels during periods of intense stress.

When I took meetings to a psych ward, there were often people in the unit with multiple years of abstinence from intoxicating substances. It is extremely humbling to have to go to a safe place when we are in crisis, but sometimes that is necessary. It is better to spend some time in a safe place than ending up using, which will only make things worse. One saying that I like is, "There is nothing so good that getting loaded can't ruin it, and nothing so bad that using can't make it worse." At least for those of us who are addicted. Spending time in lock up units is traumatic, without question, but the options can sometimes be limited. Personally, I am blessed to have a family that took me home with them, but not everyone has this opportunity. Sometimes our families can drive us crazier than the psych wards. Ideally, we can become conscious enough that we see our symptom load increasing and take action to prevent the total deterioration of our mental health. I have recently learned to do this kind of maintenance, but it has taken me years to learn my lesson.

It is important for us to also understand the people we meet might not understand when we break out in a rash of psychosis. They may think that we are neglecting them, or being rude when we are unable to communicate, or becoming upset with us that we cannot present. This stress can sometimes exacerbate the difficulties we are having. In cases like this, we can either try to explain that we need some time away, or ask for their tolerance. Communication really helps. Sometimes, people we meet later on in our recovery are startled, even scared, when we have a mental health relapse. We need to have compassion and take responsibility for our conditions and be proactive about our health, without taking on guilt about other people's concerns. It is important, though, to have a doctor to talk to, so we don't burden our friends and families with the responsibility of taking care of us.

This kind of maintenance can be tiring, but with the help of a doctor, it becomes much easier over time. Recovery from mental illness takes a tremendous amount of determination and persistence, just as recovery from any illness does. If we become overwhelmed with the burden of the dual nature of our diagnosis, we can try talking about it, writing about it, or even praying. Personally, I find great comfort walking in the hills. Being outside and breathing fresh air, seeing the natural beauty of even a small park often helps me cope when the walls are crashing around me. Sometimes we feel like we just can't relate to people. That's when the trees, birds, ocean, the hills, or any kind of natural setting can help us in a way that only nature can. Additionally, exercise has been linked to a decrease in depression. There was a study on the efficacy of medication or exercise for treating depression. Of the people tested, those who took meds did the worst, people who exercised did better, and people who exercised and took meds did the best. Getting outside can be a crucial step in turning around a serious depression. If it seems like too much of a challenge, try getting a friend to go with you. But sometimes it's best to go alone.

When we are really sick and really scared, we may be thinking that it is too hard to ask for help, or even listening when people tell us that we need it. Being under the burden of a heavy symptom load can be very embarrassing. We may wonder if there is something bad about us as people. We don't want anyone to see us in the shape that we are in, and if they do, we get very sensitive and don't want to listen. We need to have the humility to listen deeply to ourselves and those around us and have the honesty and humility to get help when we need it. It is so hard when we are compromised through our mental states or our addiction to ask for help, or even see that we need it, but we must try to learn how to identify our weak moments and take action

TENTH STEP AS RELAPSE PREVENTION

Recovery from substances, likewise, has relapse prevention models. Relapse happens first in the brain, the heart, and the mind before it manifests in using. The Tenth Step can be a good way to check with ourselves on how we are doing with our program. If we ask ourselves when the last time was that we went to a meeting or called our sponsor, we can take a quick reading of the health of our recovery. One of the first things most people who relapsed say is that they had stopped going to meetings

"MY DONKEY, MY DONKEY"

Muslims believe we will be resurrected with those we love. This applies to the Tenth Step because our ongoing inventory is a process of checking our values to see what direction we are really headed in. Sheikh Muzaffer tells a story about this:

> Once one of Jesus' apostles was preaching in a small town. The people asked him to perform a miracle, by raising the dead, as Jesus had done. They went to the town cemetery and stopped before a grave. The apostle prayed to God to bring the dead back to life. The dead man rose from his grave, looked around him and cried, "My donkey, where is my donkey?" In life he had been a poor man whose most cherished possession was his donkey. His donkey was the most important thing in his life. The same is true for you. Whatever you care about most will determine what happens to you at Resurrection. You will be together in the hereafter with those you love.[1]

---

1. Ozak, *Love is the Wine*, 13-14.

The point of including this story at this point is about the ongoing work of real change. If we continue to hold onto bad habits and bad influences, we will return to our old ways. To really change we have to seek our new playmates and new playthings. When we are given a new life, we have to become attached to new ideas and ways of being in the world, or we will just return to where we came from. Relapse is usually based on not wanting to give up our addiction or old mental health challenges that are causing our problems.

MINDFULNESS AND STEP TEN

One of the most important things to think about recovery is how close we are to using. An honest assessment of how close we are to our recovery relative to our addiction can prevent a relapse. Become aware! We can do this at the end of our day in a number of ways. We can ask ourselves if we stayed abstinent today. Some other questions that we can ask ourselves: Were we mindful today? Did we hurt anyone today? Another good way to take an inventory is briefly to cover the five precepts and to ask ourselves if we kept them to the best of our ability today. We can do the same thing with the Ten Commandments or any set of religious rules. Or we can simply make our own list. However, we choose to take our inventory, we take a minute at the end of the day to be mindful of our actions and check in with ourselves.

Ihsan: Step Eleven

> The man again asked, "O Allah's Apostle What is Ihsan (i.e. perfection
> or Benevolence)?" The Prophet said, "Ihsan is to worship Allah as if
> you see Him, and if you do not achieve this state of devotion, then
> (take it for granted that) Allah sees you."
> -SAYING OF PROPHET MUHAMMAD (PBUH)

THE ELEVENTH STEP SAYS, "We sought through prayer and meditation
to achieve conscious contact with God and to pray only for knowledge of
God's will for us and the power to carry that out." My sponsor told me a
long time ago that this is the only step that you can really practice out of
order, that it's never too soon to start doing the Eleventh Step. That's good
news because most of us have a way to go until we can do it anywhere near
in the right spirit.

Many of us seek the spiritual for the wrong reasons. We want people
to think we are really nice and to like us because we are so spiritual. We
want everyone to know how spiritual we are, so we tell everyone about our
new meditation practice or how much we have been praying. Then, after
we get all the 'oohs and the aahs' for how spiritual we are, we stop doing it.
If we are doing spiritual practice for the right reasons, we won't tell a lot of
people about it. We will do it to make less of a big deal out of ourselves, not
to make ourselves bigger and full of ego. When we seek to know God's will
for us, and have the power to carry that out, we seek to humble ourselves
even more than we have at any point in the steps. We become aware that

there are spiritual principles which are much bigger than our little agendas and egos, and we try to practice them instead of serving our own egos.

Meditation and prayer are lifelong practices. The Dalai Lama says in *Transforming the Mind*, "Whatever forms of meditation practice, the most important point is to apply mindfulness continuously, and make a sustained effort. It is unrealistic to expect results from meditation within a short period of time. What is required is continuous sustained effort."[1]

If prayer for knowledge of a Higher Power's will seems less appealing than the "ask and you shall receive method" and you are orienting around a Judeo-Christian God, think of this. Jesus said, "Are not five sparrows sold for two pennies? Yet not one of them is forgotten by God. Indeed, the very hairs of your head are all numbered. Don't be afraid; you are worth more than many sparrows." (Luke 12: 4-7; Matt 10:28-31)

And again:

> Then Jesus said to his disciples: Therefore, I tell you, do not worry about your life, what you will eat; or about your body, what you will wear. For life is more than food, and the body more than clothes. Consider the ravens: They do not sow or reap, they have no storeroom or barn; yet God feeds them. And how much more valuable you are than birds! Who of you by worrying can add a single hour to your life? Since you cannot do this very little thing, why do you worry about the rest? Consider how the wild flowers grow. They do not labor or spin. Yet I tell you, not even Solomon in all his splendor was dressed like one of these. If that is how God clothes the grass of the field, which is here today, and tomorrow is thrown into the fire, how much more will he clothe you—you of little faith! And do not set your heart on what you will eat or drink; do not worry about it. For the pagan world runs after all such things, and your Father knows that you need them. But seek his kingdom, and these things will be given to you as well. (Luke 12:22-31; Matt 6:25-33)

In other words, asking for God's will is like asking for all our needs to be provided for perfectly, to be perfectly taken care of, if we choose to appeal to Higher Power. Sometimes it's hard for me to be higher powered, but ultimately, I'm always the happiest when I am.

---

1. Dalai Lama, *Transforming the Mind*, 13.

IHSAN

One of the signs of spiritual practice is to do the right thing when no people are watching and no people can see you. The idea that God sees us at all times is part of the reason for this, what in Islam is called *ihsan*. Being spiritual and following God's will at the higher levels of practice, what we are reaching for by Step Eleven, requires this awareness. Understanding that following God's will for us is something we need to do 24/7 because of God's constant presence and love for us is a basic foundation of seeking God's will. Conscious contact with God is in a sense this understanding that we are in the presence of God at all times and cultivating a connection to this reality. If we worship God as if God sees us at all times, then every action in our lives becomes informed by this awareness.

IF IT ISN'T PRACTICAL, IT ISN'T SPIRITUAL

With the understanding that we are seeking conscious contact with God, it's understandable that people turn to scripture and seek guidance and clarity. However, one of the problems people get into with religion is that it often becomes sort of delusional. For example, when I was very sick, I read Revelations and decided I was going to bind the devil and cast him into the abyss. So, I knotted up some string and put it in a stuffed pumpkin. These types of moments are unfortunately fairly common, why psychiatrists and doctors have historically frowned on religion as a bad influence on people's sanity. Honestly, to this day when I read the Book of Revelations and the books of the prophets in the Old Testament, I get kind of paranoid. This type of paranoia has historically even been the basis for cults that have caused the death of quite a few people.

One of the antidotes to this type of insanity is the simple test of practicality. Living a quiet life and being productive is the essence of spirituality in some senses. As the hadith says, "Part of the beauty of man's religion is to leave that which does not concern him." The Bible says it differently, but it is the same sentiment. One of my favorite verses in the Bible reads, "Make it your ambition to lead a quiet life: You should mind your own business and work with your hands." (1 Thessalonians 4:11) Make it your ambition to lead a quiet life, to mind your own business, is in some ways a core principle of recovery. I am not saying to neglect politics, or not to worry about the state of the world, because these issues affect us all, but binding the devil, or figuring out too much about the rapture, the beast from the earth, the Antichrist, in some ways these concerns are extremely impractical.

Being concerned with living a life of recovery involves being concerned with treating people with dignity and respect, living a life where we take care of our mental health, and making sure that our addiction and mental illness do not negatively impact our families and friends.

GOOD ORDERLY DIRECTION

Another part of the direction that practicality and spirituality are inextricably joined is the old saying that another meaning for GOD is Good Orderly Direction. This means keeping an even keel, taking care of our mental, emotional, physical, relational, financial, and social health, and being productive members of society, living a good life. This means that we don't launch off into paranoid and counterproductive endeavors that take away from our ability to be OK in our lives as they are. Whether this means making good financial choices, or making good choices in our marriages or relationships, it often is based on having the patience to let things develop as they will with faith in God's guiding hand. Doing the next right thing is often the best choice that we can make in life. Whether it means at the end of a long day, letting go of worry and stress and just brushing our teeth and heading to sleep, or whether it means just getting out of the bed in the morning and going to work like we are scheduled to, good orderly direction means doing the next right thing, and staying in the present moment.

This is in a sense part of loving the present. Being willing to live the life we are in with gratitude and humility is important, and a core spiritual principle. Letting go of the thought that we actually know what is best for us, and being willing to trust God's will for us, we can stop straining to be like other people, have what they have, or feel insecure or inadequate because we have less money, property, and prestige than them. Recovery has been defined as living a productive satisfying life worth living, and this can happen, and in a way that is not competitive with other people's accomplishments. It's really easy to judge our insides by other people's outsides, but this just is not spiritual. Trusting God means we can be satisfied with what God has given us.

Additionally, it means using scripture as a means to humble ourselves before God and not become arrogant about how we are superior. It is really easy to read the Quran or the Bible and get caught up in how, now that we are so spiritual, all those people who we disagree with, who live their lives differently from us, or whose choices we don't agree with are hypocrites headed straight to the fire. It's easy to sit in your favorite chair and pore over scripture, complacent in the fact that our lives are pretty together now, and assured that God has forgiven and forgotten our mistakes and misdeeds and that we're just plain superior to other people, those damned and corrupt and awful people who disrespect us, or irritate us with their choices or behavior. This is simply not the purpose of scripture.

The purpose of scripture as a means to spirituality is to humble ourselves before God, and become smaller and meeker, and more loving, not more prideful, judgmental, self-satisfied and complacent. The verses we see in the Bible about hypocrisy shouldn't be a means to justify how far more righteous we are. In Islam there is the belief that God is the only one who is entitled to be proud and arrogant. It simply isn't something that is permitted for human beings. With this in mind, we can read scripture with the goal to correct our own mistakes, and not judge other people.

SOUGHT THROUGH PRAYER AND MEDITATION

The idea of seeking God's will through prayer and meditation requires something from us. It requires an effort on our part to seek guidance from our conscience, from our trusted advisors and friends, from scriptures that speak to us, and from other sources of guidance. We have to do the required seeking to get the answers. There is a practice in Buddhism called walking the question that is really powerful that I try to use often. It means you calm your mind and ask your heart a question and see what comes up. You can also thumb through or open trustworthy books for answers. Seeking guidance is like exercise: it's obvious, healthy, and you have to put in the effort.

IMPROVING CONSCIOUS CONTACT

The Eleventh Step is about building a relationship with the God of our understanding. It is important that we take the time to develop a relationship with God that is meaningful. I have often said that God is my best friend, and I truly believe this. In fact, I think God is every believer's best friend whether we know it or not. This relationship needs to be nurtured like any friendship, and it can happen in a wide variety of ways. Quiet time with

God through walking in nature, reading scripture, prayer, meditation—there are countless ways to develop a closer friendship with God.

WITH GOD AS WE UNDERSTOOD GOD

Part of getting to have a relationship with God is about building an understanding of God that is true to us. And while this, like much of what I have said in this book, might be intuitive to the point of redundancy, the importance of having faith in one's own personal relationship to God is a key part of developing conscious contact. God, as creator of the universe, is incredibly large and vast. To think that anyone can comprehend God's nature is delusional. We each have a unique perspective on what God is like. However, it is emphasized in recovery that the God of our understanding be loving, caring, and forgiving.

SALAAT

One of the five pillars of Islam is the five times daily prayer. There are endless spiritual and esoteric meanings of *salat*, but the main one for me is that it is a way to be constantly mindful of God in day-to-day life. The prayer is a source of solace for the believers. The Quran says, "And seek aid in steadfast patience and prayer: and this, indeed, is a hard thing for all but the humble in spirit, who know with certainty that they shall meet their Sustainer and that unto Him they shall return." (Quran 2:45-246) And again, "O You who have attained to faith! Seek aid in steadfast patience and prayer: for, behold, God is with those who are patient in adversity . . . " (Quran 2:153) According to the Quran prayer protects us from immorality, certainly good for anyone in recovery. The Quran says, "Convey [unto others] whatever of this divine writ has been revealed unto thee, and be constant in prayer: for, behold, prayer restrains [man] from loathsome deeds and from all that runs counter to reason; and remembrance of God is indeed the greatest [good]. And God knows all that you do." (Quran 29:45) Overall prayer is mentioned over 60 times in the Quran.[2]

There is a widespread criticism of some schools of Sufism because they have a rather loose affiliation with Islam, and they have left the prayer.

---

2. Ahmed Abdulla, "67+ Salah Quotes in Quran: Verses in Quran about Islamic Prayers."

Really, many Muslims think that once you leave behind the *salat*, you are no longer a Muslim. For some, this has been conflated with a criticism of Sufism. However, there is no doubt that most Sufis observe the five daily prayers. My experience of learning the prayer actually came before I attended a masjid, from a book on Sufism which I have already cited, called *The Illuminated Prayer: The Five-times Prayer of the Sufis as Revealed by Jellaludin Rumi and Bawa Muhaiyadeen* by Barks and Green. This book contains complete instructions for how to perform the five times prayer, as well as many inspiring quotes and beautiful pictures. You can also find instructions on prayer in Dr. Robert Frager's wonderful book *Heart, Self, and Soul* which is much easier to obtain as *The Illuminated Prayer* is out of print.[3]

I struggle with prayer on an ongoing basis. The dawn prayer is one I miss regularly, a clear sign of hypocrisy to many Muslims, and a big sin. It is said that what God loves most is prayers on time, and I am seriously lacking in this regard. However, I do my best, and I believe this is really all we can ask of ourselves, or for that matter, all that God asks of us. Establishing prayer is a lifelong process. If you are just getting started, one of the best pieces of advice is to go slow, and build gradually. Don't go so slow that you don't go, but don't go so fast that you get overwhelmed and give up either.

PURIFICATION: BEING CLEAN

Part of the path of Sufism, like the path of the Twelve Steps is purification. "Purification of the heart cleanses the heart of the distractions of everyday events and helps to concentrate on understanding the reality of the Divine."[4] There is inner purification and outer purification. In Sufism, the outer purification supports the inner, and the inner supports the outer.

The main way to obtain outer purification in Islam is through ablutions. There are minor ablutions and major ablutions, and both are described in the Quran. The major purification consists of a shower, and the minor purification is called *wudu*, and consists of washing the hands, face, and feet in a prescribed ritual pattern.[5] The above-mentioned book, *The Illuminated Prayer* contains the instructions that first taught me how to make

3. Frager, *Heart, Self, and Soul*, 173-174.

4. Angha, *Principles of Sufism*, 26.

5. You can find directions for *wudu* in Dr. Robert Frager's excellent book *Heart, Self, and Soul* on page 172.

wudu, but if you go to any mosque in the world, you will be welcomed by people who will be happy to instruct you in person. It is really very simple.

Another major form of purification that I take refuge in is reading the Quran. These two forms of worship, *wudu* and Quran, I once heard at a Friday sermon, and I never forgot it. If you read the Quran and make *wudu*, it will transform your life for the better. The Quran is a healing, a light and a guidance, and can change your heart for the better, whether in translation or in the original, whether you listen to it on iTunes or YouTube, or a CD. The Quran's healing power reaches far beyond the words, into a mystical and magical realm that goes into the secret heart of God. "Read the Holy Quran so you can find the cure to all your troubles."[6] I share these two tools with you as they have profoundly transformed my life, and if we are seeking to improve conscious contact with the God of our understanding, can make the process faster, stronger, and better.

The cleanliness of the heart comes from reflection, which is a process built into the steps, and repentance, as already discussed. "Outward cleanliness is attained with water: inner cleanliness is achieved through repentance."[7] The process of the steps, with the repentance of cleaning up our lives is a process of purification. That is part of why it is called cleaning up, and being clean.

DHIKR

Remembrance of God, and mindfulness of God, also extend beyond the prayer, or informal practices of self-reflection. There are many forms of meditation in Islam. Over the course of this text, I have discussed spiritual traditions ranging from Hinduism to Goddess worship to Christianity to Buddhism. Each of these traditions contains a variety of meditation practices. For each of us, it is necessary to follow the meditation practice which suits our spiritual path. Obviously, someone who believes in Hinduism might chant, "Om Namaha Shivaya," but that might be inappropriate for someone who is trying to get closer to Jesus. Christians might want to sit quietly and recite the name of Jesus in their hearts and wait to hear what the universe brings. This is known as the prayer of the heart and was popular among the early Christians in the deserts, ascetics who left everything to pursue their faith.

6. Ozak, *Love is the Wine*, 43.

7. Angha, *Principles of Sufism*, 34.

In Islam, and particularly in Sufism, there are many kinds of mindful-ness practices and forms of mediation. One of the main ones that I practice is *dhikr*. *Dhikr*, translated in the Quran that I use as mindfulness, is the remembrance of God. By saying the name of God in Arabic, in a variety of phrases, the practice is a way to purify the heart and refocus the mind. It is an energetic cleaning of the mirror of the heart. The Sufi understanding of the heart is that over time, the heart takes on sins, and forgetfulness and begins to accumulate black spots and rust. *Dhikr* cleans this rust off.

Dhikr is a central part of the Islamic religion, and it is mentioned in the Quran multiple times. The Quran states "remember God - standing and sitting and lying down." (Quran 4:103) The remembrance of God is a source of strength and peace. As the Quran states, "Verily in the remem-brance of God do hearts find rest." (Quran13:28) Also, "remembrance of God is indeed the greatest [good]." (Quran 29:45) And the Sufi saint Abd al-Qadir al-Jilani states, "For those who see the truth, remembrance of God is an obligation." [8]

In Islam there are 99 names of God in Arabic. Part of *dhikr* for me is chanting the names of God, either a series or one at a time. Repeating each of the names of God has special properties and qualities according to Sufis, and different names brings us closer to God in friendship. There are good names to repeat when we feel alone in addiction or in mental illness and feel people cannot understand us, as we all can sense that God understands. A beautiful book on the 99 Names of God was written by Shayk Tosun Bayrak al-Jerrahi al-Helveti, *The Name and the Named: The Divine Attributes of God.*[9]

How can you hope to have knowledge of God's will if you do not think about God, or meditate on God? Who are we to say that we love God but spend no quality time with God? If God is indeed our friend, then we need to cultivate a close and constant relationship with God to understand God and what God wants for us. One of the main ways to do this in Islam is *dhikr*. Dr. Amelia Pryor states that the idea of remembering God appears over fifty times in the Quran: "Through the *zekr*, or remembrance, we may transform our awareness, gradually and consistently, until we see the light of Allah in every direction."[10]

8. al-Qadir al-Jilani, *Secret of Secrets*, 47.

9. Bayrak, *The Name and the Named.*

10. Hammerle, Ali, Newman, and Pryor, *Sufi Grace*, 101.

The key to meditation is essentially what we have been talking about all along: mindfulness. Mindfulness allows us to work with the present moment and actually to hear what begins as the tiny voice of our Higher Power whispering to us about how maybe that load of negativity we dumped on our friend wasn't quite the right thing to do. Okay. So now we know, and we pray for the power to follow our Higher Power's will for us and not to be quite so vehement about our bad trips when someone just asked us how our day was! The Eleventh Step is a conversation. We integrate mindfulness and prayer into our lives so that our lives become vehicles of our Higher Power's will in the world. This does not mean that we all have to run off and convert to fundamentalist religion or become monastics. In fact, quite the opposite. We wake up to be more mindful, going to meetings and listening to others deeply, emptying the litter box for the cats, or taking out the garbage on trash night. Life becomes richer when we actually wake up and live it and let go of our little trips. It becomes a vehicle for learning how to heal ourselves and our world right now, right here, working at the café, sitting in rehab, talking to our families at dinner.

When I was in my addiction, there was a point when life felt like a movie. Nothing felt real anymore. Everything had become a step removed from actual lived experience. If I cut my finger, it was like watching someone else bleed. For me now, with the tools of mindfulness, life is the rich fabric that I move through (in my not so psychotic days) in a constant dialogue. It's like being a child again, when everything is vivid and fresh. Mindfulness through prayer and meditation on what our Higher Power wants for us—not what our ego, or our whimsy says will fix us—is a tool for living life to the fullest.

Recovery is a lifelong process. There is an old saying that if you don't like what recovery has given you, you can get your mystery refunded. I, for one, would rather take life on life's terms in accordance with reality than escape into the haze of avoidance characterized by mental dysfunction and the use of drugs. When trouble hits, there are two scriptures from the Bible which helped me. I will share them with you here. One is Jeremiah 29:11. My mother used to quote this to me at the worst moments of my life. She has it taped to her computer, and when I was hospitalized and at my sickest, at times of the smallest flickering light of hope, she would remind me of it. In Jeremiah God says, "For I know the plans I have for you," declares the Lord, "plans to prosper you and not to harm you, plans to give you hope and a future." (Jeremiah 29:11) The other scripture which gives me comfort in times of despair is the line from Romans which says, "And we know that in all things God works for the good of those who love him, who have been called according to his purpose." (Romans 8:28)

When we first begin to work the Twelve Steps, when we first begin to confront the task of working towards recovery from chronic illness, the task can seem overwhelming. Especially if we are hit with some sort of life difficulty in the middle of the process such as the end of the relationship, or the death of a loved one, it can seem like more than we can bear. I personally believe that we are each given the tools that we need to handle the process. We each have within us all the strength and power and courage that we need to overcome the obstacles which lie on the path between us and a free and wonderful life. Whether we choose pure mindfulness as our spiritual path, or a theistic approach combined with mindfulness, or the pure approach of prayer and faith, we will each discover within ourselves the reservoirs of energy we need to fight through to health and sustainable life.

Prayer and mindfulness are ancient tools that have empowered people for many thousands of years. One of the things that makes us human is our desire to make meaning out of a seemingly random universe. Yet, is it random? When we look at the perfection of the natural world, the minute adjustments of the forces of nature which have made life possible, the miracle of evolution, the fragile wonder of the brain, so many of us question how it all happened. For many, the modern world has lost the sense of wonder with the miracle of being. Through prayer and meditation, we can reconnect with the exquisite nature of reality. If we question whether or not there is a plan in the universe, then we can look at the delicate mechanisms of nature, so perfectly balanced, and perhaps think again.

Steps Eleven and Twelve are crucial to ongoing recovery. Meditation and prayer form the foundation of a conscious connection to our spiritual roots. Whether we worship God, Goddess, Nature, Buddha, Krishna, Allah, or Yoda, we need to take time to center ourselves in our hearts and fill up our spiritual reservoirs on a regular basis. Praying only for knowledge of our higher powers will for us and the power to carry that out is the ultimate act of humility; we accept that we don't always know just what's best and set out to do the next right thing, in a spirit of faith. The next right thing is often Step Twelve.

"THAT THEY MIGHT REFLECT"

One of the most important parts of developing a connection to God as we understand God is to take the time to meditate and contemplate who God is to us. This can happen in the context of walking in nature, and observing the birds, waters, and plants. It can happen as we spend time cooking, or being with friends and family. It can happen if we take time to just go sit in a local masjid, temple, or church, or other holy place, and just think quietly about our life, reflecting on the lessons we have learned and what we know.

Often, as people living with a mental illness, we judge ourselves for our reflections, as hallucinating or tripping out. But in reality, this may be why in ancient societies those who are mentally ill today would have been healers or shamans in the past. The time we spend thinking about God is useful and important for understanding who God is, and in turn, who we are.

WALKING THE QUESTION

There is a Buddhist mindfulness practice which is useful for developing conscious contact with a Higher Power called walking the questions.[11] It involves quietly asking one's heart a question and with an open mind just waiting to see what comes up. You can do it while walking quietly and mindfully, which is ideal, but I also often do it at my desk at work, or while driving. Just gently bring the question to mind and ask it in your mind, and be open to the answers. After you get an answer, ask again, and be open to other answers coming up. You can keep asking for twenty minutes or an hour and get a lot of different answers. The wide range of answers often brings clarity to questions that we might not right away have.

11. I learned this on retreat from Philip Moffit. He has a wonderful website where you can learn more about his work at www.dharmawisdom.org.

Chapter Twelve

SERVICE: Step Twelve

> It is better to give than to receive.
> -ACTS 20:35

STEP TWELVE STATES, "Having had a spiritual awakening as the result of these steps, we try to carry this message to addicts, alcoholics, or other sufferers of our addiction and to practice these principles in all our affairs." Carrying a message of recovery and practicing the principles of recovery in all our affairs is often the same thing. Practicing the principles in all our affairs is an act of service. Imagine if all the dope fiends you saw at meetings were loaded and all the havoc we wreak! We're doing good just by being clean to begin with. And the rest of the principles allowed us to live a different life, to follow our dreams, and not to be so caught up in all our little schemes and plans.

We need to live a spiritual life to practice Step Twelve. Spirituality is not about gathering up a bunch of spiritual ideas, becoming really educated, and reading a lot of books. Spirituality is about living differently. Living differently is characterized by service, above all else. We can be of service in a variety of ways. One way is to take care of ourselves and our mental health and not to burden our families by neglecting our responsibilities to ourselves, thereby burdening them. If we make a commitment to be present for the people in our lives, we can be of great service. Sometimes the most healing thing that we can do for people is simply to be present, be mindful of the people around us, the people sharing their lives with us. So many people just want someone to care enough to listen deeply. When we practice the principles of recovery, we are capable of this act of love.

RIGHT LIVELIHOOD

Living a life of service can extend to our employment, as it should. In our work, and our day to day lives, we can practice a spirit of service in our livelihood. Every form of work can be an act of service, from serving coffee, to being a CEO of a major company. Service is an attitude that can make every livelihood sacred.

THE BODHISATTVA VOW

There is a beautiful tradition in Buddhism that at some point in your practice, you can take a vow to become a bodhisattva. The vow is to attain enlightenment for the benefits of all beings and continue to remain in the cycle of existence until literally every blade of grass is enlightened. In other words, we don't just do this for ourselves: we do it for everyone, and we do it forever.

Bodhisattvas observed at seven *paramitas,* or practices. They are carefulness, attentiveness, patience, endeavor, meditative concentration, wisdom, and dedication.[1] I took the bodhisattva vow when I was institutionalized, and I got my hands on the Dalai Lama's book *A Flash of Lightning in the Dark of Night.*[2] Obviously, I have a long way to go until I reach enlightenment, or I observe all the *paramitas* anywhere near the level that would even come close to that of a Bodhisattva! But I mention them because they are a goal that I have for myself in the future. When you take the vow, you ask all the Bodhisattvas and Buddhas to help you attain enlightenment and keep your vows. I don't know if they took me seriously; I was vowing to them all alone in my room in the mental hospital totally hallucinating out

1. Trungpa, *Cutting through Spiritual Materialism* has a discussion of the paramitas as does the Dalai Lama in *Flash of Lightning in the Dark of Night.*
2. Dalai Lama, *Flash of Lightning in the Dark of Night.*

of my mind. But I do remember taking the vow, and I take it seriously. I just have a few lifetimes to go before I get close to the goal.

BACK TO PATIENCE: SABR

One of the most important qualities to take with you at all times on the journey of recovery and on any spiritual path is patience. The Twelve Steps take work, and for a lot of people they take a lot of time. I have only worked all twelve steps end to end two times, and I have been clean over twenty years. Additionally, often in recovery we find that we have slipped back into old ways of being that are destructive, and we have to renew our commitment to recovery. I have the sad confession that I was hospitalized for mental illness after over a decade clean. At that time in my life, I had friends and family that supported me, and I was able to turn my life back around; in fact, it was a turning point in my recovery that changed my whole life for the better. But it has been for me, with my mental health a very long, very rough, and very tiring journey.

In a sense, the reason for writing this book is the hope that others can benefit from my experience, and perhaps avoid some of the pitfalls and mistakes, and benefit from the lessons I have learned over the years. It is challenging and isolating to have a mental illness. Oftentimes, people don't like us, they shun us, we don't fit in, and we don't feel welcome. It is scary to hear what we hear and know sometimes, and it can take everything we have just to keep facing life a day at a time. And of course, the beauty of understanding that we suffer from mental difference rather than mental illness is the idea that everyone is different in their own way, and everyone suffers from some degree of mental pain and anguish, merely as the result of being human.

The patience it requires to persist on the spiritual path is often commented on by Sufis in a variety of ways. One helpful idea is that patience is a source of strength. Faith in God means that we believe that there's a plan and we can have hope. As the Quran says "Only the disbelievers, despair of God's mercy." (Quran 12: 87) The Quran repeatedly calls for the need for patience, and it is an essential tool for spiritual growth. As said already, it is part of the Bodhisattva Path as well. It is part of the eightfold path in the concept of right effort. Dr. Angha states:

> The disciplining of one's *nafs* is indispensable to the practice of patience, and this discipline is achieved through lessening the grip

on the self of the chains of desires, while at the same time setting praiseworthy goals for one's life. Working to achieve those goals assists in striving to avoid low qualities and base manners, while advancing one's knowledge and skill so that one can become a valuable and peaceful member of society. Such practices demand patience and inward dedication, but the rewards are rich: becoming an outstanding individual is helpful to one's own life as well as to the betterment of other members of the human race.[3]

To practice the spiritual principles of recovery in all our affairs takes a lifelong effort. It is the process of seeking self-understanding, self-purification, and wisdom and it leads to a life worth living, a life where we can be responsible, productive members of society.

CHARITY

Charity is one of the five pillars of Islam, and a central part of the religion. Charity is also part of Buddhism, Christianity, Judaism, Hinduism, and a moral life as understood by most people of conscience in the modern world regardless of whether or not they are religious.

SERVICE AND CARRYING THE MESSAGE OF RECOVERY

Spiritual practice is just that, practice. We practice and practice. We keep working on it. Step Twelve says we work on our spiritual practice in all our affairs. And one way we do this is by trying to serve the needs of those people who are seeking healing, who have not been on the road as long, or have fallen beside us. In doing so, we can strengthen ourselves and heal our world. We don't have to confine being spiritual just to our little circle of the world. Many people who are in recovery go out into the world and live whole lives of service. The goal is to practice both the principles that we have established in the previous steps, and our ongoing surrender to those spiritual roots over a long period of time.

We all have spiritual aspirations. There are very few people on the planet who don't have some kind of desire to be better at something. For me, I would like to be super spiritual and wake up earlier. But I struggle every day to get out of bed. The idea is that I practice getting up earlier and don't give up.

3. Angha, *Principles of Sufism*, 43.

LOVING FOR OTHERS WHAT YOU LOVE FOR YOURSELF

One of the gifts of recovery is that we are able to share the blessings we have found with other people. Living a principled life helps other people live better. We share the gifts that we have found in recovery on a day-to-day basis by carrying a message of hope with our lives.

Conclusion

ARE INSANITY, ADDICTION, MENTAL DIFFERENCE a sane reaction to an insane situation? Possibly, the reason addicts used, and left societal norms, was our perception that the fundamental explanations and reasoning that we were presented as children was flawed, warped, and dysfunctional. With the conviction that there was something drastically wrong with society as it is, we sought a way out.

Feminists in the Western European tradition have theorized that this fundamental flaw in society is based on dualistic mindsets that have been the basis for societal organizations for millennia. Theories about how this mindset originated exist, but the consensus among feminists is unanimous that the relationship of humanity to gender and sexuality, reproduction, and the body is at the core of the problem.

Many people have criticized Christianity as being the vehicle through which this dualism has been sustained. The concept is centered in a critique of the fact that in Christianity men and women exist in a hierarchical relationship where God rules over men, and men rule over women and humanity rules over nature, in a descending order of dominant hierarchies that deny agency and power in increasing degrees down the ladder of spiritual value.

On an individual basis this has been expressed in a radical alienation from the body. The dualism of mind against body, the battle between the flesh and the spirit, have both contributed to violence between people, as well as violence of individuals against themselves. In a sense, addiction is a violence against the body in that by ingesting drugs we are rejecting and manipulating sensation out of an inability to relax into life as it is.

Arguably, Islam does not have the same investment in the dualistic mindsets that have been central to Western European thinking. The centering of society around a hierarchy of men over women, with women representing an ontologically inferior other in relationship to the ontologically superior male subject is not present in Islam due to the fact that all people are in direct unmediated relationship to the Divine. The concept that men and women and nature are all autonomous responsible subjects is a basic consequence of Islamic monotheism.

Regardless of whether Islam represents a spiritual tradition that poses an alternative to Western European dualism, the reconciling of our life as embodied beings, as unified mind/body persons, represents an essential element in the development of a sustainable life in recovery. Being able to solve the tensions and vicissitudes of life without resorting to substance uses, or checking out in mental illness requires finding ways to be in the body, to unify the body and the mind in order to experience life in an integrated way without suffering in misery due to the intolerably splitting off of the experience of life with its sorrows, stress, and difficulties.

In this respect, the Islamic tradition presents concrete practices which ground the body and center the spirit in the concrete and sensual experience of life while integrating the transcendent realities of spirit

LOVE

The heart of the spiritual path, and the Sufi path, when it comes down to the final analysis, cannot merely be accessed with books, learning, or even exterior teachers, sponsors, doctors, therapists, or *shayks*. The heart of the spiritual path is a relationship to the present moment and the immanent and ever-present Divine Consciousness that is based on love. This love for God is the core foundation of Sufism, and of all monotheism, in fact of all theism. It is the ultimate journey towards the Divine. Imam Khorasani taught that the religion of Islam is about one thing: Love. Nothing matters if you really love, other than how well and how fully you love. That is the essence of the Sufi path, and of all religions.

Becoming mindful of our power to change the world increases our power to change the world, and then we have to again become mindful. This process never ends. It has to begin with yourself; that is what the steps are all about. This never-ending process is embodied in the way recovering addicts work the steps repeatedly from One to Twelve and then back to

One again. I personally am starting the steps over right now. I felt that it was possible that my experience might help people on the road who were new to the journey. The main reason that I wrote this text was that in my experiences with recovery from mental illness, I have felt marginalized so many times due to my spirituality. The term religiosity, so prevalent in psychiatric circles, has been thrown at me by therapists, psychiatrists, and my own family members who are themselves churchgoers. It is difficult to deal with the pejorative way that we as mentally different are seen by those who do not have our challenges, when we want to seek spiritual solutions.

IN A SPIRIT OF SERVICE

When I originally wrote this book in 2002, there was a need for it. As I sit here this morning working on the final bits of the book, I have received an email from the drug counseling organization that I have been a member of since 2013. The email reported the grim and heartbreaking news from the CDC that overdose deaths from April 2019 to April 2020 for the first time topped 100,000 deaths in a 12-month period, an increase of 30% from the previous year. It has been my intention and heartfelt wish to serve God as a believer for as long as I can remember, becoming more and more explicit and intentional as I have gotten older, and in my work with the homeless and mentally ill as a social worker, more and more closely acquainted with the suffering and pain of so many people in my community. I do not want to come across as writing this from ego, nor do I presume to be unique in my commitment to serving God, as most of us hold that intention. If you have not yet committed your life to serve God in love for the Creator and the Creation, I invite you to do so, with a simple prayer or intention. It is for all of us as humans. This is the *Bodhisattva* path, and it is also the path of all people who love God.

In the sense, that this is not about my ego, or claims to authority or specialness; it is important to refer you to other good books on the topic of Islam and recovery. One of the best new books that has come out is *Overcoming Addiction: An Islamic Approach to Recovery: 12 Steps for the Muslim and the Muslim Addiction Recovery Program* published by the Tayba Foundation.[1] The book, released only recently in 2021, is an excellent complement to this book. There are other resources on Islam and addiction like the Twelve Step program for Muslims, Millati Islami, who you can find

1. Adisa and Steiner, *Overcoming Addiction: An Islamic Approach to Recovery.*

on the web at www.millatiislami.org. I strongly encourage you to seek out resources, and if the spirit moves you, to begin to write your own books. We do not know what will be the key for someone to escape from a life of addiction to the freedom of recovery, and with the vast suffering in our world from addiction, it is a situation where we need all hands on deck.

A SUGGESTED PROGRAM

One of the important parts of the Twelve Steps is that it is not a list of requirements. The dogma of Twelve Steps is that it is a suggested program. Most of us have objected to the hierarchy in the world and in some ways tried to escape or rebel through our choice to use drugs, or drop out of society. Coming to recovery and expecting people to scrabble up a ladder of social success in recovery is antithetical to the way most of us think, and part of this is that recovery is entirely up to each individual. For myself, I have gone against the dogma, more than once, and sometimes paid the price. But the point of recovery is to regain our freedom, not to sacrifice it again on an altar of conformity to Twelve Steps, or religious rules and strictures. In that spirit, I am not attempting to exert any authority, or tell anyone how to live, what to think, or what to do. These are just thoughts, ideas, and suggestions of what has worked for me. If it helps, great. If it seems unhelpful, or incorrect, please disagree, don't listen to that part, or form your own opinion.

TAKE WHAT YOU NEED AND LEAVE THE REST

Probably, many people will say when they read this that I don't have the right to say what I've said, due to religious authority, or scholastic authority. This is not meant to be an academic text. But reading the text, I know that perhaps some people can benefit, and if the people who are suffering so much from mental illness and addiction benefit then this was worth it. I do not claim to be a spiritual authority. I do not claim to be the most perfect or enlightened person, but this writing is meant as a way to share my experience, so maybe I can help people. As the saying goes in recovery, "Take what you need and leave the rest." I hope that perhaps something I said in this text made you smile, or perhaps encouraged you in some way. I do not know if it has been of any use. But if it has, I thank all the bodhisattvas and Buddhas who were listening to my vow 25 years ago for it. And, of course, our amazing and powerful and ever loving, ever merciful, most wonderful, most magnificent, most beloved, God. If I have offered anything in this book you have benefited from, truly it is from God not from me, and I ask your forgiveness for the many mistakes and shortcomings in this book, which are entirely mine. May this book be of benefit to those suffering from the dual disorders of addiction and mental illness, their families and loved ones. I have faith in your power to recover and flourish, and much love and respect for you all.

Bibliography

Abd al-Qadir al-Jilani. *The Secret of Secrets: Hadrat Abd al-Qadir al-Jilani*. Translated by Tosun Bayrak. Cambridge, England: The Islamic Texts Society, 1992.

Abdulla, Ahmed. "67+ Salah Quotes in Quran: Verses in Quran about Islamic Prayers." (2021). Accessed November 1, 2021. https://myislam.org/verses-in-quran-about-salah/

'Ali Thanawi, Mawlana Ashraf. *The Accepted Whispers: Munajat-e-Maqbul*. Translated and commentary by Khalid Baig. Garden Grove, CA: openmind, 2005.

Angha, Nahid. *Principles of Sufism*. Fremont, CA: Asian Humanities, 1991.

Anonymous. *Dhammapada*. Translated by John Ross Carter and Mahinda Palihawadana. New York: Oxford University Press, 1987.

Badri, Malik B. *Islam and Alcholism*: Brentwood, MD: American Trust Publications, 1976.

Barks, Coleman, and Michael Green. *The Illuminated Prayer: The Five-Times Prayer of the Sufis as Revealed by Jellaludin Rumi and Bawa Muhaiyadeen*. New York: Ballantine, 2000.

Bayrak, Tosun. *The Name and the Named: The Divine Attributes of God*. Louisville, KT: Fons Vitae, 2006.

Baring, Anne, and Jules Cashford. *The Myth of the Goddess*. London, England: Arcana, Penguin, 1991.

Benoit, Hubert. *Zen and the Psychology of Transformation*. Rochester, Vermont: Inner Traditions International, 1990.

Berryman, Phillip. *Liberation Theology*. New York: Pantheon, 1987.

Chodron, Pema. *Start Where You Are*. Boston: Massachusetts: Shambhala, 1994.

Chomsky, Noam. *What Uncle Sam Really Wants*. Berkeley: Odonian, 1992.

Dalai Lama. *A Flash of Lightning in the Dark of Night*. Boston, MA: Shambala, 1992.

———.*Ethics for a New Millennium*. New York: Riverhead, 1999.

———.*Transforming the Mind*. London: Thorson's, Gammersmith, 2000.

Davies, Paul. *God and the New Physics*. New York: Simon and Schuster, 1984.

Davis, George W. "Sufism from its Origins to Al-Ghazzali." *The Muslim World (Hartford)* 38, no. 4 (1948): 241-256. https://doi.org/10.1111/j.1478-1913.1948.tb00983.x

Eisler, Riane. *The Chalice and the Blade*. New York: Harper, 1995.

Frager, Robert. *Heart, Self, and Soul: The Sufi Psychology of Growth, Balance, and Harmony*. Wheaton, Illinois: Quest, 1999.

Freud, Sigmund. *The Freud Reader*. Edited by Peter Gay. New York: W. W. Norton and Company, 1989.

Bibliography

Grant, Sean et al. "Mindfulness-based Relapse Prevention for Substance Use Disorders: A Systematic Review and Meta-Analysis." *Journal of Addiction Medicine*, 11, no. 5 (2017): 386-396. https://doi:10.1097/ADM.0000000000000338

Guttierrez, Gustavo. *We Drink from Our Own Wells*. Maryknoll, New York: Orbis, 1994.

Hammerle, Arife Ellen, Ali, Safa, Newman, Michael, and Amelia Pryor. *Sufi Grace: Sacred Wisdom: Heart to Heart*. Bloomington, IN. International Association of Sufism, 2009.

Hanh, Thich Nhat. *Living Buddha, Living Christ*. New York: Riverhead, 1995.

Hawkings, Stephen. *A Brief History of Time*. New York: Bantam, 1996.

Helminski, Camille. *Women of Sufism: A Hidden Treasure*. Boston: Shambhala, 2003.

Helminski, Kabir. *Living Presence: The Sufi Path to Mindfulness and the Essential Self*. New York, NY: TarcherPerigee, 2017.

Isgandarova, Nazila. "Muraqaba as a Mindfulness-based Therapy in Islamic Psychotherapy." *Journal of Religion and Health*, 58, no. 4 (2019): 1146-1160. https://doi.org/10.1007/S10943-018-0695-Y

Jonas, Hans. *The Gnostic Religion*. Boston: Beacon, 2001.

Jung, Carl, G. *The Basic Writings of C.G. Jung*. Edited by Violet Staub de Laszlo. New York: The Modern Library, 1993.

Kalupahana, David. *A History of Buddhist Philosophy*. Honolulu: University of Hawaii Press, 1992.

Khorasani, Mehdi. *Poetry of Love*. Fairfax, CA: Islamic Society of California, 2002.

———. *The Way of Success and Happiness*. Bolinas, CA: Islamic Society of California, 2000.

Lorde, Audre. *Sister Outsider*, Berkeley, CA: Crossing Press, 1984.

Office of the Surgeon General (US). *Mental Health: Culture, Race, and Ethnicity: A Supplement to Mental Health: A Report of the Surgeon General*. Rockville (MD): National Institute of Mental Health (US), 2001.

Ozak, Muzaffer. *Love is the Wine: Talks of a Sufi Master in America*. Edited by Raqib Frager al-Jerrahi al-Halveti). Chino Valley, AZ: Hohm, 2009.

Rahula, Walpola. *What the Buddha Taught*. New York: Grove, 1974.

Ruiz, Don Carlos. *The Four Agreements: A Practical Guide for Personal Freedom*. San Rafael, California: Amber Allen, 1997.

Smith, Huston, and Phil Novak. *Buddhism: A Concise Introduction*. New York: HarperCollins, 2004.

Tillich, Paul. *The Ground of Being: Neglected Essays of Paul Tillich*. Edited by Robert Price. Mindvendor, 2015.

Trungpa, Chogyam. *Cutting through Spiritual Materialism*. Berkeley: Shambhala, 1973.

Wilber, Ken. *The Marriage of Sense and Soul*. New York: Broadway, 1998.

———. *The Spectrum of Consciousness*. Wheaton, Illinois: Quest, 1993.

Witkiewitz, Katie, Greenfield, Brenna, and Sarah Bowen. "Mindfulness-based relapse prevention with racial and ethnic minority women." *Addictive Behaviors*, 38, no. 12 (2013): 2821-2824. https://doi.org/10.1016/j.addbeh.2013.08.018

www.ingramcontent.com/pod-product-compliance
Lightning Source LLC
Chambersburg PA
CBHW071442090426
42737CB00011B/1749